THE

PENTECOSTAL PULPIT

Studies in the Art of Preaching

BY KEN CHANT

"If one but tell a thing well, it moves on
with undying voice, and over the fruitful
earth and across the sea goes the bright
gleam of deeds ever unconquerable."
- Pindar (c. 518 - c. 438 BC), "Isthmian Odes" IV, l. 67

THE PENTECOSTAL PULPIT

Studies in the art of preaching

By Dr. Ken Chant

Copyright © 2012 Ken Chant

ISBN 978-1-61529-050-5

Vision Publishing
1672 Main St. E 109
Ramona, CA 92065
1-800-9-VISION
www.booksbyvision.com

All rights reserved worldwide

A NOTE ON GENDER

It is unfortunate that the English language does not contain an adequate generic pronoun (especially in the singular number) that includes without bias both male and female. So *"he, him, his, man, mankind,"* with their plurals, must do the work for both sexes. Accordingly, wherever it is appropriate to do so in the following pages, please include the feminine gender in the masculine, and vice versa.

FOOTNOTES

A work once fully referenced will thereafter be noted either by "ibid" or "op. cit."

Table of Contents

ABBREVIATIONS

Abbreviations commonly used for the books of the Bible are

Genesis	Ge	Habakkuk	Hb
Exodus	Ex	Zephaniah	Zp
Leviticus	Le	Haggai	Hg
Numbers	Nu	Zechariah	Zc
Deuteronomy	De	Malachi	Mal
Joshua	Js		
Judges	Jg		
Ruth	Ru	Matthew	Mt
1 Samuel	1 Sa	Mark	Mk
2 Samuel	2 Sa	Luke	Lu
1 Kings	1 Kg	John	Jn
2 Kings	2 Kg	Acts	Ac
1 Chronicles	1 Ch	Romans	Ro
2 Chronicles	2 Ch	1 Corinthians	1 Co
Ezra	Ezr	2 Corinthians	2 Co
Nehemiah	Ne	Galatians	Ga
Esther	Es	Ephesians	Ep
Job	Jb	Philippians	Ph
Psalm	Ps	Colossians	Cl
Proverbs	Pr	1 Thessalonians	1 Th
Ecclesiastes	Ec	2 Thessalonians	2 Th
Song of Songs	Ca *	1 Timothy	1 Ti
Isaiah	Is	2 Timothy	2 Ti
Jeremiah	Je	Titus	Tit
Lamentations	La	Philemon	Phm
Ezekiel	Ez	Hebrews	He
Daniel	Da	James	Ja
Hosea	Ho	1 Peter	1 Pe
Joel	Jl	2 Peter	2 Pe
Amos	Am	1 John	1 Jn
Obadiah	Ob	2 John	2 Jn
Jonah	Jo	3 John	3 Jn
Micah	Mi	Jude	Ju
Nahum	Na	Revelation	Re

Unless otherwise noted the scripture translations are my own.
Ca is an abbreviation of Canticles, a derivative of the Latin name of the
Song of Solomon, which is sometimes also called the Song of Songs.

PREFACE

A PIECE OF ENCOURAGEMENT

One of the most influential spiritual leaders in England during the early 17th century was a divine by the name of Laurence Chaderton. He is remembered mostly now as a scholar and as one of the translators of the *King James Version* of the Bible. But in his own time he was most famous for his preaching. For 50 years he preached nearly every Sunday in the same church to enthralled crowds. Such a remarkable career was certainly not foreseen in his childhood. He was born into a wealthy Roman Catholic family, and became a Protestant only after he had left home to go to Cambridge University. His father, deeply angered, disinherited him, and showed his scornful expectation of the boy's ruin by sending him a beggar's bowl containing a few old copper coins. Nothing daunted, the young Laurence gained his degree, was ordained, and began his splendid ministry.

It is said that one Sunday he made a rare visit to another church, and after preaching for two hours brought his sermon to an end with the words, "I will trespass no further upon your patience." But before he could sit down, loud cries arose from all over the congregation: "For God's sake, sir, go on, go on!" So he continued for another hour, to the delight and contentment of his hearers! [1]

I have not written this book, I hasten to say, to encourage three-hour sermons (we do well today to hold the interest of a congregation for thirty minutes). But preachers might at least learn how to end a sermon with the congregation yearning for more, rather than wishing it were less!

---

1   The story is found in Thomas Fuller's Worthies of England, in the "Lancashire" chapter.

CHAPTER ONE:

BETTER THAN ANGELS

PREFACE

"The Word of God is the greatest, most necessary, and most important thing in Christendom. For the Sacraments cannot be without the Word, but the Word may well be without the Sacraments. . . . God will not allow us to rely on anything or cling to anything with our hearts that is not Christ as revealed in his Word, no matter how holy and full of the Spirit it may appear to be. . . . We must hear the Word that comes to us from without and not despise it, as some think. For God will not come to you in your private room and talk with you. It is decreed that the external Word must be preached and come first. Thereupon, after one has heard the Word and taken it to heart, the Holy Spirit comes, the proper Schoolmaster, and gives power to the Word, so that it strikes root. . . .

Thus Martin Luther - who knew something about the matter - gave an extraordinary primacy to the Word of God, and especially to the preaching of scripture in church. He then insisted that nothing else could protect the church so adequately from wild enthusiasms and ruinous heresies -

"On this (primacy of scripture) we must insist, in order to protect ourselves against . . . those muddle-headed enthusiasts . . . who boast that they have the Spirit without and before the Word, then proceed to judge, explain, and stretch Scripture or the spoken Word as they please. . . . These all are those who, apart from the use of the means of grace, reckon to devour the Holy Spirit, feathers and all, and are spiritualized through and through. . . . Many splendid words . . . they prate, so that he who does not know the devil might think they have five Holy Spirits with them. But when you ask them: How does one obtain this exalted Spirit? they do not direct you to the outward Gospel but to a utopia and say: Stand awaiting, as I have stood, then you will experience it; the heavenly voice will come, and God himself will speak with you. . . . Do you not see the devil, that enemy of divine order, in this method? How he gets you to gape with the words: Spirit, Spirit, Spirit! . . .

And then, in perhaps the highest encomium ever given to the preaching office, Luther declared he would rather go to church and hear a sermon than see some heavenly vision!

"Even if we heard angels preach in their majesty, we would not be moved any more by it than we are now by hearing our pastor or other ministers preach. If we were sure that what we hear is the Word of God, we would not snore so and be so lazy and secure. But because we think mere men are speaking and that it is man's word that we hear, we become unreasonable beasts. . . . Indeed, if the matter were in my hands, I would not want God to speak to me from heaven or to appear to me. But I would want - and this is my daily prayer - that I might . . . see and hear the brethren, who have grace and the Holy Spirit, and who by the Word can console, strengthen, exhort, admonish, and teach me. What better and more useful appearance of God would you desire? [2]

Would that be *your* choice? Would you prefer a sermon to an angelic visitation? Can it really be better to listen to a preacher than to have God speak to you from heaven? Is there truly no greater appearance of God in the church than you can find in a sermon preached in the grace of Christ and inspired by the Holy Spirit?

As it happens, long before I knew Martin Luther's opinion on the matter, I had come to the same conclusion myself. I have never craved "visions", but oh! how joyous to encounter great exposition of scripture!

---

2   What Luther Says, compiled by Ewald M. Plass; Concordia Publishing House, St Louis,1959; Vol Two, selections #2858, 2863, 2865, 2868, 2873, 2875. Abbreviated and slightly paraphrased.

Even if Luther's sentiments were a little extreme, it would do the church no harm to absorb them again. In these days, when so many chase only fluff and feathers, we need to recapture the biblical notion that ***nothing stands higher in the church than the pulpit*** - not prayer, not worship, not the sacraments, not visions of angels, not prophesyings, nor anything else. You may take almost everything away from a church, and it will survive; but banish the pulpit, and it will soon perish. Now the pulpit means preachers, and preachers mean sermons. These pages, then, are about preachers and their sermons, and how the two should come together to build the church of Jesus Christ.

THE HIGHEST CALLING

If you don't think much of Martin Luther, then listen to a higher authority. In the most solemn terms Paul impressed upon young Timothy the urgent importance of preaching (2 Ti 4:1,2,5). Unless faithful preaching is maintained, a drought far worse than any merely natural disaster will bring famine upon the church and bring a dearth upon all the land (Am 8:11). Let us then say something about what it means to be a preacher.

THE CHRISTIAN EXCALIBUR

"Preaching is the manifestation of the incarnate Word, from the written Word, by the spoken word" (Bernard Manning). To the extent we abandon or minimize the preaching office in the church to that extent we betray the gospel and cease to be fully Christian.

In the fables of Camelot, King Arthur was invincible so long as he wielded his magic sword Excalibur and kept its enchanted scabbard. When he drew Excalibur, the gleaming blade flashed like a blazing sun, dazzling the eyes of his enemies, and compelling them to fall before it like straw before a scythe. While he held the great sword in a true hand he could not be overthrown; but when the scabbard was stolen from him, and Excalibur betrayed, darkness soon engulfed the realm, and the beautiful dream of Camelot became a dread nightmare.

We have our own *Excalibur*, which is no legend, but the real *Sword of the Spirit*, the Word of God (Ep 6:17). To that we must cling as if our very lives depended upon it, for they do! Mark this: no church can prosper more than its pulpit prospers. Exalt anything above preaching the Word of God and fanciful delusions will soon lead the church on a bleak trek into the wilderness.

SPEAK WHAT IS PRECIOUS

The Great Commission gives first mandate to preaching (Mk 16:15). But against the world's opposition that is not always easy to fulfil, and many a preacher has been tempted to lay down a burden that has seemed too heavy to carry. Some of God's finest servants have felt that pain. For example, the prophet Jeremiah once came to loath his calling, and he decided that he would never again speak in the name of the Lord. He complained that *"his pain was never-ending, and his wounds seemed incurable."* He argued that God had treated him deceitfully, behaving like a desert mirage, or like a river without water. He accused the Lord of treachery, scathingly declaring that neither God nor his promise could be trusted (15:18). Few preachers (if any) avoid stumbling into the same place of doleful lament. But God's response was adamant. No matter how disappointed the preacher might feel, nor how much opposition the pulpit faces, nor how wrong ministry may seem to become, there is only one thing to do:

> *"Turn back, and I will take you back, and you will again stand in my presence. You will become my spokesman when you set yourself to speak only what is precious and not what is vile. Make this people turn to you, for you must never turn to them!" (vs. 19).*

That is always the choice: will the pulpit be turned around by the people, or will they be turned around by the pulpit? But whether or not the people change, God's prophet must cling to God's Word, refusing to fall silent or lose heart. Whether or not they heed our words, the demand is inflexible: *"speak only what is precious, never what is vile"* - that is, stick to preaching God's Word, the whole of his Word, and nothing but his Word. We have no higher task. We dare do no less.

JESUS WAS A PREACHER

When Jesus began his ministry, *"he came to Galilee preaching the gospel of God"* (Mk 1:14). Note how he also ended his ministry with preaching, and was known during it primarily, not as Miracle-Worker, but as Teacher (Mk 4:38; 5:35; 9:17,38; 10:17,20,35,51; 12:14,19,32; 13:1; 14:14; plus a score of other places). Christ was a preacher above all. He found himself in the Word of God; he preached about himself from the Word of God (Lu 24:27). Every person whom God has called into ministry is expected to follow the Master's example. Jesus, by his own demonstration, elevated the preaching office to the highest degree. The church cannot do any work that is more important.

PAUL WAS A PREACHER

Paul too was primarily a teacher and a theologian of genius, and he was emphatic: there can be no real faith apart from hearing the Word of God preached (Ro 10:10, 14,15). Furthermore, he makes a startling assertion about preaching: *"God in his wisdom decided that the world would never discover him through wisdom. Instead, he has chosen to bring people to faith and to salvation through the foolishness of our preaching"* (1 Co 1:21).

That statement is a mixture of good news and bad news:

- *good news, because preaching is God's ordained way of bringing people from darkness to light, and from death to life;*
- *bad news, because it tears away any pretence that preaching is a wondrously wise or clever thing.*

We preachers need to hear this, and put a knife to our besetting sin of pride. Although nothing stands higher in the church than its pulpit, do not forget that the best of us (at least by the world's measure), are prating fools, spouting nonsense. All preachers are ridiculous. Consider the matter and you will soon realize that the idea of someone getting behind a pulpit and hoping by a clumsy sermon to change the world is preposterous. What clowns we are! How few speak cleverly, how few appear winsome or wise, how few have any valid thespian skills, how few could perform in a theatre without being mocked, how few ever scale the heights of scholarship! Yet we claim a power beyond that of the most superb actors, the most stirring orators, or the most profound philosophers! Who but we reckon that their words can make the blind see, and the deaf hear, and the cripples walk, and even break the chains of death and open the locked gates of the grave? Absurd! the world cries, yet cannot deny the evidence of its own eyes. For this company of ordinary men and women, sparse in gifts, low in skills - but called by God to preach - exerts an influence that transcends natural barriers and carries people out of themselves to the very throne of God, and changes the shape of the earth!

But never forget that preaching cannot ever rise above the definition **"foolish"**. Woe to ministers who begin to think themselves important, or suppose that they are the very paragons of wisdom and genius. Weep for pastors who strut around reckoning themselves the stuff from which greatness is made. Who are we? Nobody! What are we? Nothing? What is our work? Folly! Only by the grace of God, only through the touch of Christ, can our pulpits be transformed into the portals of divine glory. Unless the Holy Spirit breathes upon us, even in our highest endeavors we are but fools preaching foolish sermons foolishly.

THE BURDEN OF THE LORD

The biblical idea of preaching is perhaps best summed up in the phrase used by the prophets: **"the burden of ...** (Is 13:1; 15:1; 17:1; 21:1,11,13; Je 23:33-38: plus many other places). A sermon should, as nearly as the preacher can achieve, represent a burden of truth that the Lord has laid upon his or her spirit, which cannot gain relief until the message is delivered (cp. Je 1:4-9; 5:14; 20:9). No one has expressed this idea better than Elihu, who gave a colorful description of a teacher whose "belly was about to burst" (Jb 32:17-22.) But behold a paradox! Are we the poorer because we empty ourselves in our preaching? Hardly! For what greater wealth can a person gain, except what comes from giving; and what greater poverty is there than to hold onto what should be cast abroad? (Lu 6:38; Pr 11:24). The more one gives out cheerfully what the Lord has dropped into the spirit, the more riches will be again restored. Or, to put it more bluntly: use it, or lose it! As Sir Thomas Wyatt wrote -

> What vaileth under kay [3]
> To keep treasure alway
> That never shall see day?
> If it be not used,
> It is but abused.
> And as for such treasure
> That maketh thee the richer,
> And no deal the poorer,

---

3   Locked away in a safe.

When it is given or lent,
Methinks it were well spent. [4]

4   Song #83, st. 4 & 8. Sir Thomas Wyatt (1503-42) was an English courtier,
diplomat, and poet.

CHAPTER TWO:

CRYING IN THE WILDERNESS

Kahlil Gibran, in his story about the prophet Almustafa, gives a picture of the yearning that should consume every preacher. Here is the ultimate pain of the preacher's "burden": so few seem willing to relieve him of the weight of his riches. In the story, the prophet is found standing alone in his garden, and he cries out -

> "Heavy-laden is my soul with her own ripe fruit. Who is there would come and take and be satisfied . . . and thus ease me of the weight of mine own abundance?

> "My soul is running over with the wine of the ages. Is there no thirsty one to come and drink?

> "Behold, there was a man standing at the cross-roads with hands stretched forth unto the passersby, and his hands were filled with jewels. And he called upon the passers-by, saying: `Pity me, and take from me. In God's name, take out of my hands and console me.'

> "But the passers-by only looked upon him, and none took out of his hand.

> "Would rather that he were a beggar stretching forth his hand to receive - ay, a shivering hand, and brought back empty to his bosom - than to stretch it forth full of rich gifts and find none to receive. . . .

"Would that I were a tree flowerless and fruitless,
For the pain of abundance is more bitter than barrenness,
And the sorrow of the rich man from whom none will take
Is greater than the grief of the beggar to whom none would give.
"Would that I were a well, dry and parched, and men throwing stones into me;
For this were better and easier to be borne than to be a source of living water

When men pass by and will not drink."[5]

What earnest preacher has not felt that grief? A hand, a heart, full of the treasures of heaven, waiting to be given generously to all who ask - yet there are few who care, few who truly listen, few who catch the visions that enrapture the preacher's soul. This is perhaps part of the cross that we are called to carry for Christ. This much is certain: if you cannot live with that pain without becoming sour, angry, embittered, then you are unfit for the pulpit. An indestructible graciousness, an unquenchable love, an unshakeable confidence, are marks of the man or the woman called by God to preach the unchangeable Word of life.

But now a question must be asked: how responsible are we for the rejection of our message? How much duty do we have to compel people to accept what we say? Must we take on the burden of persuasion as well as proclamation?

ALMOST PERSUADED

You will not find in these pages any discussion on the art of how to persuade people to respond in the way you want them to. There is undoubtedly some room for that prowess in the preacher's tool-box, but it seems to me to be over-emphasized. We are not religious equivalents of the super-salesmen of the secular world. Converts that are talked into the kingdom by a preacher can be easily enough talked out of it by the devil. [6] Only those who are persuaded by the Holy Spirit will be truly convinced, convicted, and converted. We are called primarily to be advocates not marketers, proclaimers not merchants, heralds not lobbyists, ambassadors not diplomats (2 Co 5:20).

So another question should be asked: are secular theories of persuasion truly conformable to the requirements of the Christian evangel? Should our thrust (like that of a car salesman) be entirely goal-oriented, that is, designed only to produce a stated result on earth; or should our preaching be above all a declaration of divine truth, spoken in obedience to a divine

---

5   The Garden of the Prophet; Alfred A. Knopf, New York, 1986; pg. 51-55.
6   Which is one of the main reasons for the huge discrepancy between the number of those who make so-called "decisions for Christ" in our altar calls, and those who become life-time disciples of Christ.

mandate, whatever the consequences may be? Are we focussed on results, or on truth?

NOT A SET OF TECHNIQUES

We cannot allow the pulpit to be reduced to little more than a set of coercive techniques, a methodology for statistical increase, a church version of a secular advertising agency. Our task is not to induce people to act in a certain way, but to instruct them in righteousness, and then to allow the Holy Spirit to elicit whatever response pleases him.

We have already seen in this century the terrifying effectiveness of modern techniques of persuasion, both in the political and religious worlds. Think about the "brainwashing" methods of the Nazis and their various totalitarian kin. Think about the similar techniques used by the cults, with devastating consequences. Have evangelical Christians been at least partly guilty of adopting the same kind of tactics to "persuade" people to accept Christ, or to conform in some other way to biblical requirements? If someone yields under my pressure then that person becomes my convert, and may be quickly lost again. Instead, preachers would be wiser to keep their sermons shaped only into a tool the Holy Spirit can use to accomplish the hidden purposes of the kingdom of God.

No doubt some seemingly marvelous results can be gained by using the modern apparatus of persuasion - just watch the political and commercial worlds at work winning their adherents and customers! But if we do the same, is God then building the church, or man? (Ps 127:1) Heed the fable of The Three Little pigs, and remember that our "Big Bad Wolf" can easily blow down structures of straw and sticks. Only God can build a house of bricks, able to withstand any buffeting by the enemy.

THE EXAMPLE OF PAUL

Think about Paul. Can you imagine the apostle rushing out to use manipulative techniques in order to improve his growth statistics? Notice his quite different approach to ministry -

> *"The message I preach does not depend upon clever words and shrewd argument, but upon a demonstration of the power of the Holy Spirit. I want your faith to rest, not upon human wisdom, but upon the power of God" (1 Co 2:4).*

How many of our "converts" have been persuaded by fine words, or eloquent argument, or emotional exploitation, rather than by the genuine conviction of the Holy Spirit? But who is responsible for the harvest? The preacher or the Holy Spirit? Yet there exists a deeply-rooted idea that we must carry the main burden, and therefore must endlessly struggle to make our preaching more effective, more persuasive, more appealing. What a crushing burden that has placed upon the pulpit! No wonder the land is littered with shattered pastors, exhausted, dispirited, all joy gone out of their ministry! It is a load too heavy for any preacher to carry. It turns Christian ministry into a commercial competition, a struggle for customers, an endless battle to meet a remorseless demand for numerical growth. The dominant factor then becomes, not what God wants the preacher to preach, but a crass assessment of what will most please the greatest number of people.

We are not called to obtain a certain quota of souls, but to be faithful in proclaiming the Word of God. The results do not depend upon the preacher, but upon the Holy Spirit. Paul may plant, and Apollos may water, but only God can give the kind of increase that builds his kingdom (1 Co 3:5-9). Let us then no longer focus upon achievement, but rather upon faithfulness.

GOD'S MARKET STRATEGY

Does winning the lost really depend upon the church developing right strategies, improving its marketing skills, selling its goods more shrewdly, using cunning advertisements, and employing the most effective tools of persuasion? If so, why doesn't God restrict his call to men and women who are gifted communicators? Why does he perversely continue to choose large numbers of preachers whose pulpit skills are at best modest! How few have thrilling, well-modulated voices, strong personalities, innate charisma, or a handsome appearance! Instead, God goes right on calling men and women

> "who are not wise by human standards, who do not possess powerful temperaments or noble gifts."

He prefers, in the main,

> "to choose those who are foolish in the eyes of the world to embarrass the wise, and those who are weak in the world to shame the strong, and those who have no

*standing in the world, and are scorned, to reduce to
nothing what the world thinks is important!" (1 Co 1:26-
28).*

Surely that says something about God's disdain of the things this world
and much of the church think are essential for persuasion? (vs. 20-21).

THE EXAMPLE OF JESUS

Notice how little interested Jesus was in talking anyone into faith against
their own desire. As a communicator (by modern commercial standards)
he was not very successful. He had no discernible technique, he
followed no consistent pattern. He moved easily from a comfortable chat
to denunciatory preaching. Now he is telling a charming story, but then
he bewilders his hearers with parables; now he speaks simply, but later
baffles the people with obscurity. Always he is unpredictable! You
cannot categorize Jesus nor draw from his ministry a cluster of
marketable ideas on How To Preach For Best Results! On the contrary,
he was often deliberately offensive (Mt 23:13-33). He could make the
most outlandish statements without any qualification or apology (Mk
9:43-48; Mt 5:38-42); nor did he hesitate to hide himself from people - as
he did several times during his ministry and, even after his resurrection,
on the road to Emmaus (Lu 24:13-16).

Not even the people he dealt with personally were always converted;
thus

- we do not know what happened to Nicodemus (Jn 3:1-8);

- the rich young ruler went away from Jesus disappointed
  (Lu 18:18-23);

- he often infuriated the scribes and the priests;

- even his own family wanted to lock him up! (Mk 3:21, 31)

Jesus made no attempt to solve the world's problems, he offered no easy
cures for human pain, he raised no protest against Roman tyranny -
indeed, he was apparently indifferent to the pain the nation was suffering
under the crushing heel of a foreign despot. Perhaps he represents a
better model for us to follow than any of the techniques we can gain from
the insights of modern mind-manipulators.

DO WE ABANDON ALL PERSUASION?

There is of course abundant room in preaching for exhortation, encouragement, invitation, an appeal to the heart as well as the mind, and for instruction, challenge, and the like. But it should always end where scripture ends. Not with coercion, nor manipulation, nor "pressure tactics" of any sort, but with the proffer: whoever will, may come! (Re 22:17).

Our task is to bring our hearers as nearly as we can to a full comprehension of the message of the gospel, and then to stand aside and allow them, under the influence of the Holy Spirit alone, to make their own decision about whether or not to yield to the claims of Christ. [7]

CONCLUSION

Let me bring this chapter to an end with a final warning against yielding to the temptation to attract a crowd by using emotion and novelty. Seldom are genuine disciples - that is, men and women living wholly under the lordship of Christ - made by employing such devices. Preachers whose main appeal has been emotional rather than reasonable have done fearful harm over the centuries. Here is a tragic example.

---

[7]   For several of the seed ideas in the above paragraphs on "persuasion", I am indebted to two or three magazine articles, and particularly to "The Perils of Persuasive Preaching," by A. Duane Litfin, in Christianity Today, February 4, 1977; pg. 14-17. In his turn, Dr Litfin drew upon J. I. Packer's notable book, Evangelism and the Sovereignty of God, which I first read perhaps 30 years ago. In a still earlier edition of the magazine (June 7, 1963, pg. 4), Peter H. Eldersveld wrote: "In the only sense in which `persuasion' and `edification' are theologically meaningful, they are the work of the Holy Spirit (Conrad H. Massa) . . . The sermon must be an exposition of the Word of God, not the word of man; it must come from the soul of the preacher to the soul of the hearer, as divine revelation by the power of the Spirit of God . . . Therefore it cannot be judged in terms of results according to human standards. It does not `sell' something: it does not merely seek to please people, nor to persuade them, nor even teach them or get decisions and conversions. Rather, it tries simply to let the Word of God speak, knowing that in the last analysis only God can produce the results."

The First Crusade to capture Jerusalem from the Muslims and to establish a Christian state in Palestine was launched in the 11th century, in anticipation of the Second Advent of Christ. The Crusaders firmly believed, because of Bible prophecy, that Jesus would come again one thousand years after the completion of the New Testament. They also saw in scripture that he would descend first upon the city of Jerusalem. But how could this happen while Jerusalem was occupied by Muslims? So there was a sense of urgency about planting a Christian banner on Mount Zion. The "last days" were surely upon them, and they had the sacred task of preparing the way for the returning King.

One of the popular preachers who went around stirring up enthusiasm for the Crusade was Peter the Hermit. A contemporary chronicler, Guibert of Nogent, says that

> "he was surrounded by such throngs of people, given such gifts, acclaimed as such an example of holiness, that I remember no one ever having been held in such honor. ... Indeed, whatever he did or said seemed almost godlike, to such a degree that hairs were pulled from his mule as relics. We report this not for love of truth, but to show the common people's love of novelty."

So tens of thousands marched off to war, ill-trained, ill-equipped, and unfit for battle. Despite their pious enthusiasm they were slaughtered en masse. Another chronicler says that

> "when the scattered remains of the slaughtered men were collected, they made not merely a hill or mound or peak, but a huge mountain, deep and wide, most remarkable, so great was the pile of bones." [8]

We might observe that nothing much has changed. People are still hungry for novelty, they still yield ignorantly to persuasive preaching, and the end result is still bleached bones. Do not allow yourself to become a partner in such folly.

---

8   From Chronicles of the Crusades; ed. Elizabeth Hallam; Weidenfeld and Nicolson, London, 1989; pg. 65, 68.

CHAPTER THREE :

SINCERELY YOURS

One of the greatest artists of the Italian Renaissance was a painter known simply as Giotto (1266-1337). His fame reached the ears of Pope Benedict IX, who was planning to commission some paintings for St Peter's -

> "(The Pope) sent one his courtiers . . . to find out what sort of man Giotto was and what his work was like. On his way to see Giotto and to find out whether there were other masters in Florence who could do skilful work in painting and mosaic, this courtier spoke to many artists in Sienna. He took some of their drawings and then went on to Florence itself, where one day he arrived at Giotto's workshop to find the artist at work. The courtier told Giotto what the Pope had in mind and the way in which he wanted to make use of his services, and, finally, he asked Giotto for a drawing which he could send to his Holiness. At this Giotto, who was a very courteous man, took a sheet of paper and a brush dipped in red, closed his arm to his side, so as to make a sort of compass of it, and then, with a twist of his hand drew such a perfect circle that it was a marvel to see. Then, with a smile, he said to the courier: `There's your drawing.'

> "As if he were being ridiculed, the courtier replied: `Is this the only drawing I'm to have?'

> "`It's more than enough,' answered Giotto.  `Send it along with the others and you'll see whether it's understood or not.'

> "The Pope's messenger, seeing that was all he was going to get, went away very dissatisfied, convinced he had been made a fool of. All the same, when he sent the Pope the other drawings and the names of those who had

done them, he also sent the one by Giotto, explaining the way Giotto had drawn the circle without moving his arm and without the help of a compass.

"This showed the Pope and a number of knowledgeable courtiers how much Giotto surpassed all the other painters of that time." [9]

The courtier misunderstood the true qualifications required of a great painter, especially one who was called to decorate a magnificent church. The mistake is still being made. Men and women are often chosen for some office, or given high acclaim, for the wrong reasons. Like the pope's messenger, we frequently overlook the simple, the pure, the truly necessary skills, and are overawed by mere color and splash. What then are the prime qualifications we should expect in a preacher?

THE CALL OF GOD

See Jeremiah 23:21-22. If God has not sent you, do not run. If God has not spoken to you, do not prophesy. Christian ministry is not a task for the self-appointed, but only for those who have been chosen, called, anointed, and equipped by the Lord. Even so, certain aspects of character may, and should, be looked for by the church -

PERSONAL QUALITIES

1. HOLINESS

(a) At once let us dismiss any thought of a self-made holiness. Though there is certainly work for us to do, and sometimes hard work, we cannot build any righteous status before God by our own toil. Holiness, true heavenly holiness, can be inwrought only by the Holy Spirit. God has no patience with a sweaty priesthood (Ez 44:18). He does indeed want holy servants, but they must be made holy by his own gift and gracious working in Christ (Ro 5:15-17), not by their zealous efforts. No one's labor

---

9   Giorfio Vasari (1511-1574), Lives of the Artists, tr. by George Bull; The Folio Society,London, 1993; in three volumes; Vol. One, pg. 44,45, "The Life of Giotto."

can add any value to the imparted merits of Christ; no one's faults can diminish those merits in the slightest.

(b) Holiness, then, for a Christian, is not marked by abstinence from certain pleasures, nor by doing certain good works, but rather by an utter dependence upon Christ (Ga 2:20). He is the Guide and Guardian of our lives. Without him we are nothing, we have nothing, and we can do nothing that holds the slightest value within the kingdom of God.

When Beethoven completed his glorious Ninth Symphony (the Choral) in 1823 he had already been completely deaf for several years. Nonetheless he conducted its first performance himself, in Vienna. Unknown to him another conductor sat out of sight, whom the orchestra actually followed while pretending to watch the composer. The plan worked well, and when the symphony came to its thrilling end the audience tumultuously acclaimed the great work. Despite the thunderous applause, Beethoven was unaware the music had stopped, and knew nothing about his success until one of the singers took him by the hand and turned him around. Only then did he realize that his masterpiece was receiving a standing ovation, but that another hand had directed the performance.

We are like that. If our hidden Conductor is not there, our performance must become a shambles. Yet he wants us to take the podium and to receive the acclaim for a job well done. But when the crowd is clapping you, remember whose hand held the real baton!

(c) Holiness, however, does not arise merely from a dependence upon Christ, but also requires a focus upon him; or, as Paul puts it, "in everything Christ must have pre-eminence" (Cl 1:18).

"If we love doctrine more than Christ, we are rationalists. If we love forms or ceremonies more than Christ, we are ritualists. If we love our works more than Christ, we are legalists. If we love the local aspect of the assembly more than Christ, we are sectarians. If we love our experiences more than Christ, we are emotionalists." [10]

---

10   W. E. Best, No Proper Name; published by the author; pg. 14.

That is why John abruptly ends his first letter with the strange words, Little children, keep yourselves from idols." One of his meanings, as the previous verses show, is that we dare not allow anything else to usurp the supreme place Christ holds in our affections. He must be the ultimate goal of all preaching, as well as the true source of it. To depart from that standard is to depart from holiness, and therefore to become disqualified for the task.

(d) The great 18th century Shakespearean actor David Garrick once said that he would give 100 guineas [11] to be able to say "Oh!" like George Whitfield, who could bring sobs of repentance to a multitude by uttering one syllable. Garrick remained disappointed, for Whitfield's power came not from mere histrionics, but from holiness. I do not mean that any saintly preacher can become an irresistible orator; but that without holiness, inwrought first and then outwrought, no preacher can fulfil his or her divine office.

2. SINCERITY

(a) Thomas Carlyle, on Robert Burns (1759-96):

"The excellence of Burns is, indeed, among the rarest, whether in poetry or prose; but at the same time, it is plain and easily recognised: his Sincerity, his indisputable air of Truth. Here are no fabulous joys or woes; no hollow fantastic sentimentalities; no wiredrawn refinings, either in thought or feeling: the passion that is traced before us has glowed in a living heart; the opinion he utters has risen from his understanding, and been a light to his own steps. He does not write from hearsay, but from sight and experience; it is the scene that he has lived and labored amidst, that he describes: those scenes, rude and humble as they are, have kindled beautiful emotions in his soul, noble thoughts, and definite resolves; and he speaks forth what is in him, not from any outward call of vanity or interest, but because his heart is too full to be silent. He speaks it with such

---

11 At least two years' wages for a skilled artisan in those days.

melody and modulation as he can; `in homely rustic jingle'; but it is his own, and genuine.

"This is the grand secret for finding readers and retaining them: let him who would move and convince others, be first moved and convinced himself. Horace's rule, `Si vis me flere ... ' [12] is applicable in a wider sense than the literal one. To every poet, to every writer, we might say: Be true, if you would be believed. Let a man but speak with genuine earnestness the thought, the emotion, the actual condition of his own heart, and other men - so strangely are we all knit together by the tie of sympathy - must and will give heed to him ... for in spite of all casual varieties in outward rank or inward, as face answers to face, so does the heart of man to man." [13]

What was true of an 18th century Scottish poet should be even more true of 20th century preachers. We cannot hope to be believed if we are not true.

(b) Likewise, consider this moving passage from Henry David Thoreau

"We talk of genius as if it were a mere knack, and the poet could only express what other men conceived. But in comparison with his task, the poet is the least talented of any; the writer of prose has more skill. See what talent the smith has. His material is pliant in his hands. When the poet is most inspired, is stimulated by an aura which never even colors the afternoons of common men, then his talent is all gone, and he is no longer a poet. The gods do not grant him any skill more than another. They never put their gifts into his hands, but they encompass and sustain him with their breath ... "

In a mysterious way, says Thoreau, those who are naturally able to write poetry are the least gifted of mortals, they are not poets at all. Poetry

12 The full quotation is from Ars Poetica and reads: "If you wish to draw tears from me, you must first feel pain yourself."

13 From a mid-19th century essay by Carlyle on Robert Burns.

deserves the name only when it arises, not from some human genius, but from a divine seed planted in the poet's soul. The poet's words then become only a transcription of a heavenly song. Whatever natural talent the poet may have had, is utterly subsumed in the glory of the Muse. A similar idea was expressed even earlier, by Pindar -

> "I have many swift arrows in my quiver which speak to the wise, but for the crowd they need interpreters. The skilled poet is one who knows much through natural gift, but those who have merely learned their art chatter turbulently, vainly, against the divine bird of Zeus." [14]

One of the ways to recognize a true heavenly inspiration, Thoreau continued, is to observe the poet's life. If it remains unchanged by his poetry, then he is merely playing a game with words. True poetry cannot be just the product of a writer's mind, but the very stuff of the poet's daily conduct; then and then alone does it deserve the honoured title -.

> "The true poem is not that which the public read. There is always a poem not printed on paper, coincident with the production of this, stereotyped in the poet's life. It is what he has become through his work. Not, how is the idea expressed in stone, or on canvas or paper, is the question, but how far has it obtained form and expression in the life of the artist. His true work will not stand in any prince's gallery.
>
> `My life has been the poem I would have writ,
> But I could not both live and utter it.*
>
> `I hearing get, who had but ears,
> And sight, who had but eyes before,*
>
> I moments live, who lived but years,
> And truth discern, who knew but learning's lore.' " [15]

---

14 Olympian Odes II, l. 150. Pindar was the chief lyric poet of ancient Greece. Zeus was the supreme deity of the Greek mythical pantheon.

15 A Week On The Concord and Merrimac Rivers; The Heritage Press, CT, 1975 edition; pg279, 280, 285. The second poem comes, according to some, from some lines from Ossian, a legendary Gaelic poet.

Could the nature of preaching be better described? Change "poet" to "preacher", and you will discover the very essence of what we should be and what our task is. No sermon can be greater than the character of the preacher, nor can any words speak louder than his or her life.

3. ENTHUSIASM

Notice how the above passages inescapably link sincerity with enthusiasm (that is, heartfelt emotion). The two are truly inseparable. Thus Robert Graves writes:

> "Two hundred years ago a bishop approached the famous British actor David Garrick and inquired why clergymen `though believing what they preached, met with little response, while Garrick, knowing his subject to be only a fable, could rouse his audience.'

> "Garrick replied that actors deliver their fictions with the warmth and energy of truth while ministers `pronounce the most solemn truths with as much coldness and languor as if they were the most trivial fictions.'

> "Garrick was not suggesting that preachers be trained in theatrics, but that they deliver a living message with life ... Dwight Moody once wished his associate pastor could spend five minutes in hell. He knew such an experience would excite and motivate the most reserved preacher." [16]

But let enthusiasm be tempered by self control, otherwise you might earn the indictment against a preacher given in 1887 by Richard Blackmore: [17] "(I found myself) sitting under the most furious dustman that ever thumped a cushion."

4. TRANSPARENCY

Another mark of sincerity is **transparency** - that is, that you are what you appear to be, not working to a hidden agenda, not saying one thing while meaning another, not playing the part of a hypocrite. The public and private lives of a preacher should be fully conformed to each other,

16   From an article Preaching in the August 1986 "Advance" magazine.
17   An English novelist, most famous for Lorna Doone.

disclosing the same face at home as at church, neither more nor less pious in one place than the other, but the same everywhere and at all times. Such consistency used to be taken for granted. Now there is a sorry trend for people to wear two characters: one for pious public display; the other for private use alone.

In one his poems John Donne (1572-1631) praises the Countess of Bedford, warmly commending her for her unblurred character, and likening her life to a temple built out of "specular stone". This was thought to be a perfectly transparent substance, used long ago by the ancients but now lost. Legend held that many temples were built from it, so that everything happening inside was fully visible to all who passed by. The poet describes the countess as having the same quality of openness to every eye -

> This, as an amber drop enwraps a bee,
> Covering discovers your quick soul; that we
> May in your through-shine front your heart's thoughts see.
> You teach (though we learn not) a thing unknown
> To our late times, the use of specular stone,
> Through which all things within without were shown.
> Of such were temples; so and such you are . . . "

And such should you and I be, especially if we claim the right to proclaim the truth in Christ.

CHAPTER FOUR:

BORROWED MOCCASINS

No doubt you have heard the saying, "You cannot condemn another man until you have walked a mile in his moccasins." Whatever truth those words may have in law, [18] they are certainly true in ministry. A sermon must come out of the heart, not just the head; it must be born from life, not just from thought. Basil Hart [19] captured the same idea -

> "Keep strong, if possible. In any case, keep cool. [20] Have unlimited patience. Never corner an opponent, and always assist him to save his face. Put yourself in his shoes - so as to see things through his eyes. Avoid self-righteousness like the devil - nothing is so self-binding."

Here, then, we look at some of the ways of achieving those admirable aims.

EXPERIENCE

The general rule is this: **preach only what you have personally experienced**; for example, the comfort of God to console the bereaved; the power of God to deliver the sinner; and so on. Whatever moccasins your sermon wears, you hearers should sense that you yourself have walked many miles in them. But how is that possible? How can any one preacher enter into the gamut of human laughter and tears, triumph and defeat, riches and poverty, love and hate? Can it be done at all? Yes! There are 3 ways to gain this personal experience.

1. IMMEDIATELY

Paul knew that he had earned the right comfort other people in their trials, because he himself had experienced the comfort of God -

---

18   They underlie the rule of trial by a jury of our peers.
19   About whom I know nothing, except the above quote.
20   Echoes of 2 Ti 4:5! *"As for you, always stay calm, put up with suffering, do the work of an evangelist, and fulfil all the demands of your ministry."*

> *"God consoles us in all our troubles so that we can turn around and offer solace to others when they are in trouble. We can share with them the consolation that we ourselves have received from God. . . . If we have to suffer pain, it is a price we are willing to pay so that you can be consoled; and if we find our own comfort in God, it is just so that we can help you to find similar comfort. You will also discover the strength to face bravely the very same sufferings that we are experiencing" (2 Co 1:3-6).*

So the ordinary events of daily life, the things that happen to everybody, are one of God's ways to equip preachers to minister effectively to other people.

2. VICARIOUSLY

There are three ways to widen one's experience vicariously. **First**, through counseling other people, and thus entering sympathetically into their experience of life, with all its delights and traumas. **Second**, through the intimate association of deep friendship, and through the discovery that comes out of close fellowship with other Christians. Something of what your friends are, and of what they have felt, is inescapably communicated through the channels of love. **Third**, good literature and fine poetry are an excellent source of vicarious experience of life, especially poetry -

> "So it is not an accident that a large body of poetry fills the central part of the Hebrew scriptures, with seventeen books of history on one side, and seventeen books of prophecy on the other. This layout suggests that if one knows only history and theology, then one's life and ministry will be incomplete.

> "I think that every pastor and preacher should read poetry - not just the Psalms, but a wide range of poetry. It would imbue them with a deeper sensitivity to the human condition, it would save them from numerous

follies I have observed over the years, it would immeasurably enrich their lives." [21]

"People who do not acquire and keep bright the love of poetry draw far less joy from life than those who do. Joseph Conrad once said that many travellers come back from their journeys having gained little more than the labels on their suitcases. Such, for all too many people, is the journey through life. They go here, they do this and that, but none of it leaves much impression. But to the mind nurtured on poetry, life becomes more significant, recollections of beautiful things become sharper, experience becomes deeper and wider. Poetry helps to create a keen awareness of life." [22]

3. SCRIPTURALLY

No book better reveals the human condition than the Bible. Its pages can take you into the innermost heart of kings and commoners, prophets and peasants, the brave and the fearful, the virtuous and the wicked, and on through all classes and kinds of men and women in almost every imaginable life-situation. Yet more is needed than just a reading of the book. Through prayer and meditation the preacher needs to bring about a penetration of its message into his or her spirit. Out of that fusing of your own soul with scripture will arise sermons that are alive with reality, not merely artificial constructions. Notice how caustically Jeremiah denounced those prophets who merely aped the sermons of other preachers (Je 23:30,31,33-38; they were artificially using Isaiah's phrase "the burden of the Lord").

On this matter, hear Martin Luther again:

"Some pastors and preachers are lazy and no good. They rely on these and other good books to get a sermon out of them. They do not pray; they do not study; they do not read; they do not search the scripture. It is just as if there were no need to read the Bible for this purpose.

---

21   Songs To Live By, by Ken Chant; Vision Christian College, Sydney, 1994; pg. 8.
22   Children's Encyclopaedia, ed. Arthur Mee; Educational Book Society, London, 1963; Vol 1B, pg. 601.

They use such books as offer them homiletical helps in order to earn their yearly living; they are nothing but parrots and jackdaws, which learn to repeat without understanding . . . Therefore the call is: watch, study, attend to reading. In truth you cannot read too much in scripture; and what you read you cannot read too carefully, and what you read carefully you cannot understand too well, and what you understand well you cannot teach too well . . . He who has only one word of the Word of God and cannot preach a whole sermon on the basis of this one word is not worthy ever to preach!" [23]

Thus I once heard about an old black pastor, who preached an extraordinarily powerful sermon based entirely upon Lu 23:54, "It was only Friday, and Sunday had not yet come!." He told how the Jews, the Romans, the demons of hell, and other foes of Christ all chortled with glee when they managed to pin him to the cross. But they were laughing too soon: it was only Friday; Sunday (the day of resurrection) had not yet come! So today, the world rejoices, thinking it has overcome the church, while many churches lament, thinking Christ is dead. But in God's grand economy it is only "Friday"; his great "Sunday" is still to come! But come it will, and then the world's laughter will turn to tears, and the church that wept will sing with joy!

But now, back to the idea of gaining vicarious experience from scripture. In a pun on the old English maxim, "Take care of the pence and the pounds will take care of themselves," Lewis Carroll caused the Duchess to say, "Take care of the sense, and the sounds will take care of themselves." [24] That twisted saying is one of the many irrelevant morals the Duchess pronounced; nonetheless, it spells wisdom for a preacher. If you know your subject thoroughly you will have no difficulty telling it properly; get the sense right, and the right sounds will follow! Martin Luther spoke plainly on the same theme -

---

23 What Luther Says, vol. 3; selections 3547,3546.
24   Alice in Wonderland, Ch. 9.

"Who knows their subject can speak easily, for art follows comprehension of the subject. I can never compose a sermon by the rules of rhetoric." [25]

Those who without ceasing or wearying pour themselves into scripture, and pour the scriptures into themselves, will never lack that good "word in season", which brings such joy (Pr 15:23), and is more precious than "golden apples set in a frame of silver" (25:11). Such preachers will be able to echo the gratitude of Isaiah -

> *"The Lord God has taught me how to be a teacher, so that I may comfort the weary with a word in season. He wakes me up every morning, he sharpens my attention, so that I might be a good pupil myself, and thus fit to teach others" (Is 50:4).*

SIMPLICITY

Sincerity is often marked by plainness and simplicity, [26] not overly contrived, not aspiring to be thought clever, not trying to emulate another more successful preacher -

> "When you are going to preach, first pray and say: `Dear Lord, I would preach for thy honor; though I can do nothing good of myself, do thou make it good.' Don't think about Melancthon or Bugenhagen or me or any learned man, and don't try to be learned in the pulpit. I have never been troubled because I could not preach well, but I am overawed to think that I have to preach before God's face and speak of his infinite majesty and divine being. Therefore be strong and pray." [27]

> "Let all your sermons be very plain and simple. Think not of the prince, but of the uncultivated and ignorant people. The prince himself is made of the same stuff as they! If in my preaching I should address myself to Philip I should do no good. I preach very simply to the

---

25 Table Talk of Martin Luther, ed. Thomas Kepler, Baker Book House, 1979.
26 But not always, as you will find below, under the heading "The Whole Counsel of God."
27 Martin Luther, op. cit.

uneducated and it suits everybody. Though I know
Greek, Hebrew and Latin, these languages I keep for use
among ourselves, and then we get them so twisted that
our Lord God is amazed." [28]

However, this rule of **sincerity** does not preclude the use (with
acknowledgment, where necessary) of other material. Benjamin Franklin
in his Poor Richard's Almanack for 1746, conceded cheerfully that the
poems at the head of each month were not all his own work:

"I need not tell thee that not many of them are of my
own making. If thou hast any judgment in poetry, thou
wilt easily discern the workman from the bungler. I
know as well as thee, that I am no poet born; and it is a
trade I never learnt, nor indeed could learn. . . .

"Why then should I give my readers bad lines of my
own, when good ones of other people's are so plenty?
'Tis methinks a poor excuse for the bad entertainment of
guests, that the food we set before them, though coarse
and ordinary, is of one's own raising, off one's own
plantation, etc, when there is plenty of what is ten times
better to be had in the market." [29]

But don't rob another's work and call it your own; follow rather the
example of a renowned 17th century speaker, William Cavendish, the
Duke of Newcastle, of whom his wife said:

"He loves to intermingle his discourse with some short
pleasant stories, and witty sayings, and always names the
author from whom he hath them; for he hates to make
another man's wit his own." [30]

I have myself suffered from shameless plagiarism. On one occasion I
was teaching an all-day pastors' seminar when, halfway through the
morning, one of the men came up to me and complained angrily because

28 Ibid.
29 His Life As He Wrote It, ed. Esmond Wright; Folio Society, London, 1989;
    pg. 95-96.
30 The Grand Quarrel, ed. Roger Hudson; Folio Society, London, 1993; pg.
    15.

(he said) I had stolen another man's material. It transpired that at a gathering held three months earlier, this other preacher had presented a set of printed notes, bearing his name as the author, that were nearly identical to the ones I was using. Reasonably enough, I was accused of unscrupulously purloining his ideas. As it happens, the reverse was true! That fellow had attended one of my seminars in another city, and had copied out my studies almost word for word, with not one syllable of acknowledgment! Only with difficulty was I able to convince the seminar attendees that I was innocent! Even so, I had to restructure the remaining lectures, so that I could share with the pastors something they had not already heard.

On another occasion, I picked up a book in a church I was visiting, supposedly written by its pastor, and began to read. The words seemed strangely familiar. As I read on, slowly it dawned on me that these were my own paragraphs. That rascal had taken one of my books, changed not a line except the name of the author on the front cover, and was selling the book as his own work!

In fact, on many occasions over the years, when visiting various churches, I have come across sermon outlines, radio talks, Bible studies, booklets, and the like, that had been stolen without acknowledgment from my writings. Plagiarism, whether spoken or written, is theft! But reasonable use of copied material, with open recognition of the source, is accepted by all as fair.

1. HUMILITY

One of the marks of genuine sincerity will be a desire to keep the preacher as much out of view as possible, and the Word of God as much to the fore as possible. In the Preface to his brilliant gothic novel, The Picture of Dorian Gray, Oscar Wilde wrote -

"The artist is the creator of beautiful things.
To reveal art and conceal the artist is art's aim."

The result of a sermon (as I heard someone say somewhere) should not be the cry, "What a wonderful sermon!" but, "What a wonderful Saviour!" That may be a little idealistic, and I am myself human enough to appreciate both - that is, for the congregation to applaud my Lord and me! Nonetheless, my dearest wish, whether or not anyone remembers me or my message, is that something of Christ will be planted within them, to remain for ever.

2. FAITH

You must approach your task with unshakeable confidence in the power of the preached word to bring life and fruit. Such faith can spring only out of an equally unshakeable conviction that you are called to the task of preaching in this place at this time. There is something special about true preachers: no matter how often they fail; no matter how many embarrassing stumbles they suffer; no matter how repeatedly their message is thrown back into their teeth; no matter how regularly they are pushed under the water, they keeping bobbing back up again. They are like a rocking clown: knock them over as often as you please, immediately they jump straight up again, still smiling. Their inner assurance is almost arrogant; somehow they cannot be made to doubt that their preaching is good, and that it will sooner or later achieve its God-given purpose.

3. ANOINTING

Certain questions are often asked about "the anointing of God": how should you describe the anointing; how does one achieve it; what are the distinguishing marks of the anointing; how do you know whether or not it is on you? - etc. Know at once that an "anointing" has nothing to do with noise, sweat, rapid speech, emotion, tears, a superlative level of performance, or any other such observable phenomenon. Such things are commonly aroused in political orators, actors, athletes, gamblers, and others, who do not find it necessary to credit their surge of energy or skill to the Holy Spirit. Which does not mean that such phenomena are wrong or unnecessary, for they have their proper place in preaching as in other fields of human endeavor; but their source is natural adrenaline, not supernatural unction.

The fact is, sometimes you will feel like preaching, and sometimes you won't; sometimes you will do your job well, at other times poorly. In neither case is the true anointing of God either enhanced or diminished (Jn 14:16-17; 1 Jn 2:27).

So what should you do when you don't feel like preaching, or when everything seems to be going wrong? Panic? Rush into a couple of days of prayer and fasting? Storm heaven for a fresh unction? You might be better advised to take the same attitude as the journalist Sydney Harris did. He was addressing a group of hopeful writers, and one of them asked, "Mr Harris, what do you do when you don't feel like writing?" He replied: "I write. That's the difference between an amateur and a professional."

The popular concept of the anointing has little to do with the biblical one. In scripture, the anointing is primarily the "call of God"; that is, that act by which God sovereignly chooses a person for a particular task, and sets that person apart for that task. I either have such an anointing (call) or I don't. If I do have it, then the only thing required of me is to perform each God-given task to the best of my ability, with such obedience, prayer, faith, and toil as my particular office may require. I certainly will not waste time hunting around for some elusive, mysterious, indefinable, subjective afflatus.

If I am diligently working to fulfil all that the Father has given me to do, then I am confident that my efforts will produce the extent of "harvest" he has ordained ("some 30, some 60, some 100-fold").

As a born-again, Spirit-filled believer, called to the ministry, I am already "anointed". The only thing to be determined at the bema will be how well I have fulfilled that anointing.

CHAPTER FIVE:

HANGING ON EVERY WORD!

People who want great preaching need to be great listeners. Few congregations realize how much their preachers are influenced, even conditioned, by the behaviour of the people. A story is told about a group of university students who decided to experiment with some ideas their lecturer had been sharing with them. Whenever the lecturer moved to the right of the platform, the students gave many positive responses (nodding assent, sitting up, applause, and the like); but when he moved to the left, they showed a negative response (looking bored, yawning, stony-faced, slouching, and the like). After a few sessions, true to the lecturer's own predictions, he was unconsciously fixed to the right hand side of the platform, on the very edge!

In much the same way, whether you are aware of it or not, your audience will exert an influence over you. So the people should be taught how to listen properly to the Word of God; in any case they will get the preaching they deserve. It is indeed true -

> "Happy is any speaker who not only makes good sense,
> but also addresses an attentive audience!" (Sir 25:9).

In Aristophanes' play, The Frogs, one scene is set in Hades, where a great debate occurs between the deceased playwrights Euripides and Aeschylus. At one point the Chorus chimes in, wondering whether a modern audience (circa 400 B.C.) has the wit to understand the finer points of the debate. They decide in the affirmative, but the idea is presented that a dearth of intelligent hearing must produce a dearth of fine teaching -

> Fear ye this, that today's spectators
> Lack the grace of artistic lore,
> Lack the knowledge they need for taking
> All the points ye will soon be making?
> Fear it not: the alarm is groundless:
> That, be sure is the case no more.
> All have fought the campaign ere this:

Each a book of the words is holding;
Never a single point they'll miss.
Bright their natures, and now, I ween,
Newly wetted, and sharp, and keen.
Dread not any defect of wit.
Battle away without misgiving,
Sure that the audience, at least, are fit. [31]

I wonder, though, if the same could said of the congregation you will be addressing next Sunday? Are the people "fit" to hear and understand the Word of God? Are they good listeners? If not, the responsibility rests with us preachers to teach people the disciplines necessary for them to sit down, listen, comprehend, believe, and obey the Word of God. Preachers and congregations need each other. The preacher must do the best he (or she) can, to make his message worth hearing; the people must accept that great preaching depends upon a great audience. Both must embrace their respective disciplines, and offer their proper worship to God: one by speaking like an oracle of the Almighty (1 Pe 4:11); the other by giving the most earnest heed to the spoken Word.

But now let us turn away from the pew and back to the pulpit, for here are five things you should know about preachers -

SOME ARE MORE GIFTED THAN OTHERS

Wise preachers will be aware both of their skills, and of their weaknesses (Ro 12:3-7); God has not given us all the same abilities. Remember again the astonishing abilities of the great George Whitfield, which have seldom been equalled and probably never surpassed. Such superbly gifted orators may appear only once in each century. The same is true of the theatre -

> "No student of the theatre, no serious actress approaching the part, can entirely rid themselves of the idea that Lady McBeth should look like Romney's portrait of Mrs Siddons [32] . . . and should sound as we

---

31   Five Comedies of Aristophanes, tr. Benjamin Bickley Rogers; Doubleday Anchor Books, New York, 1955; pg. 125,126.

32   An English actress who reached the peak of her fame in the late 18th and early 19th centuries. "Endowed with a gloriously expressive and beautiful face, a queenly figure, and a voice of richest power and flexibility, she

understand that Mrs Siddons sounded. It is said that she asked a waiter to bring some mustard and the poor man fainted away, so thrilling was her tone." [33]

Sadly perhaps, but nonetheless truly, few of us can command abilities of that rare order. People may faint when you and I speak, but probably not for the same reason! Yet sometimes even those who are highly skilled as orators can be defeated by other deficiencies in their temperament or personality:

"Some people are clever enough to teach others, yet do no good for themselves. Here is a gifted speaker who keeps on making enemies, and in the end dies of hunger! Why? Because he is destitute of wisdom and the Lord withholds from him grace and charm." (Sir 37:19-21)

Some of us, of course, lose on both counts: not only do we lack remarkable public-speaking skills, we also possess abrasive character traits that often undo what good our words might have accomplished! Many have wondered why God made the terrible mistake of calling them to the pulpit! Surely he could have found someone else, far more qualified?

But even if God has not given you fulsome "grace and charm", even you are comparatively "destitute of wisdom", does that condemn you to failure? No, says Sirach in the next line, for a godly life linked with sensible teaching can make a great preacher out of anyone -

"But if someone conducts his own life well, then you may assume that he speaks good sense when he gives you advice. And the wise speaker who sensibly instructs his own people will see enduring fruit for his labour. That wise speaker will be heaped with praise, and

worked assiduously to cultivate her gifts until as a tragic actress she reached a height of perfection probably unsurpassed by any player of any age or country." (Chambers Biographical Dictionary)

33 Tyrone Guthrie, in his Preface to The Comedies Vol. One, by William Shakespeare; the Heritage Press, Norwalk CT, 1986; pg. xliv.

everyone who sees him will call him happy!" (Sir 37:19-24). [34]

In the end, none of us can do any more than accept who and what we are, change whatever is possible to change for the better, but otherwise get on with life and with ministry, utilizing such talents as we do possess. As Paul once said,

"I may not be a clever preacher, but I do have knowledge, and I have always declared to you everything that is true." [35]

FEW GET WHAT THEY THINK THEY DESERVE

You may say it is hardly fair of God to give a preacher a few skills, but then seemingly to countermand those gifts by adding a nasty cluster of personal blemishes. And then what about the injustice shown by the unequal distribution of abilities? Why should one preacher be wonderfully gifted while another has hardly any skills at all? Do not both preachers have the same duty to occupy the pulpit effectively? How can that be called fair, when it is so much easier for one than for the other, and the earthly rewards are so disparate?

Even more painful, you may be obliged to watch some who are less gifted than you are, go out and prosper more richly. Or perhaps you suffer the most severe sorrow of all? You are good enough to know what the best really is, yet must accept that for you it will always be unattainable. As the Greek lyric poet mused long ago -

"They say that this lot is the bitterest: to recognize the good, but by necessity to be barred from it." [36]

Perhaps that is your state? Like Sirach's unfortunate orator, you cannot escape some slight deficiency of skill, some missing element of style, or some defect of character or temperament, that are just enough to prevent

34   For a more extended passage, in which Sirach contrasts laborers and others with scholars, and gives a delightful description of some of the needful qualities of a successful preacher, see 38:24-39:11.

35   2 Co 11:6. He was responding to a sneering criticism reported in 10:10, "His letters may be weighty and forceful, but his physical appearance is paltry, and his preaching is contemptible."

36   Pindar (circa 518 - circa 438 B.C.), Pythian Odes IV, l. 510.

you from ever scaling the noblest peaks. Each time you feel ready to grasp the highest success it somehow slips out of your hand. How cruel it all seems!

But when since the Fall has life ever been fair? John Steinbeck, in his retelling of the stories of Camelot, describes how Sir Balin, having proved himself the only knight worthy to draw an enchanted sword from its scabbard, then discovered that a curse attached itself to any man who held the weapon. The wizard Merlin pronounced the warrior's doom -

> "The knight who drew the sword is the best and the bravest, yet the sword he has drawn will destroy him. Everything he does will turn to bitterness and death through no fault of his own. The curse of the sword has become his fate." Sir Balin cried out, "That is not fair. It is not just!" Merlin replied, "Misfortune is not fair, fate is not just, but they exist just the same." [37]

What then shall we do? Certainly not rail against an unjust providence, but rather, what every person must do: simply take what life does offer and make the best possible use of it.

> The common problem, yours, mine, every one's
> Is - not to fancy what were fair in life
> Provided it could be - but, finding first
> What may be, then find how to make it fair
> Up to our means: a very different thing! [38]

Somewhere in her exquisite novel Silas Marner, George Eliot observes how foolish it is for people to reach middle age, still restlessly craving more happiness, unable to realize that life never can be entirely joyful. A shadow of sorrow must lie over all earthly happiness. The wise know this, and make of each day the best they can, accepting the dispositions of Providence, grateful for what grace they do possess, and resolved to glorify God in every way they can.

---

37   The Acts of King Arthur and His Noble Knights; Ballantine Books, New York; 1990; pg. 71, 85.

38   From Robert Browning's poem, Bishop Blougram's Apology.

WE ALL HAVE GOOD DAYS AND BAD DAYS

Anyone can learn many of the arts of great preaching, but in the end there is a genius, which, if it is not born in you, no amount of learning or practice can impart. Yet even the most skilled will sometimes be stunned both by excellent and by abominable performances. There is little point in looking for reasons for either happening; certainly, it is absurd to be hunting for some kind of pious or spiritual explanation, as if either God or Satan were directly involved.

Sir Laurence Olivier was reckoned to be the greatest male Shakespearean actor of the 20th century, if not of all time. His dramatic powers were just as extraordinary on the screen as they were in the live theatre, so he was accustomed to receiving constant acclaim. But on one occasion he reached sensational heights in his performance, and a thunderous standing ovation shook the building as he left the stage. However, when his fellow actors and the theatre staff later crowded around him, pouring upon him their congratulations, he was curt and angry. He cursed them, pushed his way through the crowd, and rushed distraught into his dressing room. His friends were bewildered. One of them finally approached the actor and asked, "Why are you so upset? Don't you know that your acting was marvellous?" Olivier replied with despair, "Of course I know I was superb! But I don't know how or why I was able to do it. So how do I know if I can ever do it again?"

Preachers too need to accept that sometimes, for no discernible reason we will do well and at other times dismally. Nonetheless, constant practice, hard study, and diligent care will diminish the chasms and increase the peaks, so that whereas you once seldom preached a fine message, now you will seldom preach a poor one!

THERE IS ALWAYS SOME BENEFIT TO BE FOUND

No matter how poorly you have performed, God is able to work in it and through it for good (Ro 8:28). Preachers who hope for longevity must cultivate the art of focussing not upon the dross but upon the gold, of gazing upon the stars rather than the black sky. Or, to use the American maxim: look at the donut, not the hole! No sermon is so bad that it lacks all merit, nor is any situation so dire that no benefit can be found.

During the latter part of the 5th century before Christ, Athens was occasionally ruled by the tyrant Alcibiades. One evening Alcibiades blundered drunk into the home of Anytus, a wealthy citizen, just as a number of guests were about to begin a sumptuous meal. Observing the tables luxuriously set with gold and silver vessels, the tyrant ordered his slaves to carry away half of them to his own house. According to Plutarch, the dinner guests protested angrily against such arrogant violence; but Anytus replied graciously, "On the contrary, Alcibiades had shown great consideration and tenderness in taking only a part when he might have taken all."

That same optimism must characterize all who are called to serve Christ and the church. In the midst of our worst failures Christ is still at work. The devil is never permitted to carry away all our treasure! Some precious things remain, and the Holy Spirit will continue to use them for the glory of God.

WE ARE CALLED TO BE FAITHFUL, NOT CLEVER

By all means, let us be as clever as we can (I would rather, like Paul, be called a "master builder" than a bumbling fool, 1 Co 3:10); but in the end, God alone determines how much each seed produces (Mk 4:8). Furthermore, who knows what a day may bring? You may lose tomorrow all that you have today; you may gain tomorrow all that you lack today (Ja 4:13-17). As Solomon said, one man may come out of prison and find himself elevated to a throne, while another, who once ruled a multitude, may perish in obscurity (Ec 4:13-16).

That lesson has never been better exemplified than in the tragic end of Darius, who called himself "King of Kings", and once ruled the mighty Persian empire. Alexander the Great invaded his domain with a small army of less than 50,000 men. Against him Darius led a host numbering more than half a million superbly armed warriors. But Alexander thrashed him, and then again, and again. Finally Darius, left with nothing but a small dog and his chariot, was assassinated by his own fleeing nobles. As he lay dying, Polystratus, a messenger from the victorious Alexander, found him, and heard the king's last prayer -

> "'May Alexander, safe and unharmed, and raised far
> above the lot of my fortune and the envy of the gods, on

the throne of Cyrus complete a glorious life, and mindful of his own virtue, may he allow my mother and my children to have that place in his regard which they have deserved because of their loyalty and respect. But may a speedy death overtake my murderers, which Alexander will inflict upon them, if not from pity for an unhappy enemy, at least from hatred of their crimes, and for fear that, if these go unpunished, they may break out to the destruction also of other kings and even to his own.'

After these words, being tormented by thirst and being refreshed with water brought to him by Polystratus, Darius said: `So, then, this final calamity was fated to be added also to such great misfortunes ... ` Then he stretched out his right hand . . . and grasping the hand of Polystratus he gave up the ghost. Whether Alexander arrived while Darius was still breathing is uncertain; this much is sure, that on learning of the wretched end of a most powerful king, he shed many tears, and at once taking off his cloak, he covered the body, and ordered it to be taken with great honour to his family, in order to be embalmed after the fashion of the Persian kings, and placed among the tombs of his predecessors. The treachery of the men at whose hands Darius suffered a most cruel death in return for the greatest favours, although in its own nature horrifying and execrable, was marked with greater infamy for future generations by the wonderful faithfulness of a dog, which alone was with Darius when he was deserted by all his friends, and fawned upon him when he was dying as it had when he was alive.

"Such was the end of life allotted to that king whom shortly before men thought to be insulted unless they addressed him as `King of Kings' and kinsmen of the gods; and once more it was proved by a striking example, that no one is more exposed to Fortune's changes than one who, having been honoured by very

many of her favours, has bowed his neck wholly under
her yoke." [39]

So life, as James warned, is unsure for everyone, from the highest to the
lowest. Nonetheless, we should all try to bring such skills as we do have
to their fullest potential. Only a fool reckons that nothing more remains
to be learned, or that no further improvement is possible. Every day
brings a new promise, a new possibility. As long as God gives you life
and breath never allow disappointment or discouragement to deter you
from trying again, and reaching for better things.

> Thank God! There is always a Land of Beyond
> For us who are true to the trail;
> A vision to seek, a beckoning peak,
> A fairness that never will fail;
> A pride in our soul that mocks at a goal,
> A manhood that irks at a bond,
> And try how we will, unattainable still,
> Behold it, our Land of Beyond! [40]

We should be like the great Dutch painter Rembrandt. Before he reached
his mid-twenties he had already gained such fame that the Crown Prince
of Holland requested one of his paintings to add to the Royal Collection.
To have one of his works hanging in the palace would have brought the
young artist vast renown. He could then have greatly increased the
prices he asked for his work. But Rembrandt declined the prince's
invitation. When asked why, he declared that none of his paintings was
good enough, and that when the time came he would himself choose a
work that would be worthy to grace the walls of the palace. He was then
asked which one of his existing works he thought the best. At once he
thumped his chest and cried, "The one that is still there!"

Let that be your confidence, too: more of the beauty of Christ shines in
your soul than you have ever yet put into words. You have still to preach
your best sermon!

---

39   The History of Alexander Book Five, by the ancient Roman historian
     Quintus Curtius. The translator's name and publishing details are unknown
     to me.
40   Robert Service, The Land of Beyond, Stanza Three.

CHAPTER SIX:

PULPITEERING OR POWER?

"It was the best of times, it was the worst of times."

So begins Charles Dickens' famous novel, A Tale of Two Cities. Dickens, of course, was writing about London and Paris during the time of the French Revolution. His eventual hero was Sydney Carton who on the scaffold uttered the immortal lines, "It is a far, far better thing that I do than I have ever done; it is a far, far better rest that I go to, than I have ever known."

But the hero of our chapter is the apostle Paul, and the two cities are Corinth (where Paul enjoyed the best of times), and Athens (where he suffered the worst); and our story comes out of Paul's first letter to the Corinthians (2:1-5). Why did Paul - whom history has called "the lion of God" - arrive in Corinth, as he says, "drained of strength, filled with anxiety, trembling with dread"? The answer lies in following Paul's footsteps -

PAUL AT CORINTH - THE BEST OF TIMES

1. THE SUPERNATURAL CHURCH

Paul was committed to a ministry of miracles (vs. 4,5). He could not imagine preaching the gospel without accompanying "signs, wonders, and miracles" (see the entire Book of Acts, and also Ro 15:17-19; 1 Th 1:4-5; etc). For those first Christians the gospel could not be fully preached without a constant display of the supernatural; they could not suppose the church able to gather without some miracle of answered prayer.

Yet how soon they fell away from that exciting commitment! Shortly after the death of the last apostle miracles began to decline. Within one hundred years they had nearly vanished from the church, except in pockets here and there. [41] The charismatic leadership of the apostles and prophets slowly became submerged beneath the growing power of the bureaucracy, expressed through bishops and presbyters (priests). Soon nothing could be observed in the Christian assemblies beyond what human ingenuity alone could achieve, without any help from God. No longer could you see and hear things that could only have come from heaven's glory.

We observe the same decline happening in our own time. After barely one hundred years, already the genuinely supernatural is extinct in much of the Pentecostal and charismatic movements around the world. Seldom are cripples made immediately whole, or the blind given back their sight, or the deaf their hearing, or the dead their life. What began in a blaze of miracles has subsided into the confines of natural programs and methods.

Why is this so? Why are miracles so easily lost by the church? Why is it so hard to keep a firm grip upon the healing power of Christ? Why do we so readily shift from signs to programs, from wonders to hype, and from miracles to methods? The answer is clear; it is Because the church functions in -

2. THE NATURAL WORLD

The church must exist in a natural environment, where it faces two relentless foes: the powers of darkness; and a secular society. Both of those enemies loathe the supernatural and also any church that tries to demonstrate the power of God. They have plenty of reason to do so -

(a) SATAN HATES THE SUPERNATURAL

Never forget that the kingdom of darkness is itself a supernatural kingdom. The power of Satan is not physical but spiritual. The devil has no fear of technologies, programs, advertising campaigns, promotional methods, nor of any kind of social, political, or commercial strategy. We may employ as many of those tools as we please without doing much

---

41   They never entirely vanished, of course. There was the remarkable Montanist revival that broke out in the latter part of the second century, and always there were isolated groups of believers, or surges of revival from time to time, that kept the charismata alive in the church.

damage to his realm. [42] But miracles done in the name of Jesus strike at the very heart of his kingdom. He dreads the charismata (1 Co 12:7-11) planted in the church by the Holy Spirit. So he strives without resting to lock the church into a natural framework. A natural church cannot seriously threaten his hegemony; but a church full of miracles make the denizens of hell shriek in terror. If the early church "turned the world upside down" (Ac 17:6), it was mostly because

> *"everywhere they went they preached the good news, and the Lord was their co-worker, confirming their message by the miracles that accompanied it . . . Yes! God added his own testimony to theirs by signs, wonders, many different miracles, and by the gifts of the Holy Spirit" (Mk 16:20; He 2:4).*

We delude ourselves if we think there is any better way, or for that matter, any other way to reap a full harvest for Christ. If Satan can strip the miraculous from the church he can mock its pretensions to spiritual power. But let the church seize the gifts and power of the Holy Spirit and the gates of hell must soon begin to tremble! The supernatural gives the church mastery over every demon and over all the power of the enemy (Lu 10:18-19).

But if Satan hates the supernatural, we must also realize that

(b) THE WORLD HATES THE SUPERNATURAL

Contrary to popular opinion, this world loves only spurious miracles. The real signs and wonders that spring out of the gospel are anathema to secular man. Why is that so?

(i) Miracles Strike at its Natural Wisdom

How much this world loves its own wisdom! Think how much money our society spends on education, on its schools and colleges. Along with sporting stadia, this world's real temples are its universities. Knowledge is a wonderful thing, and by all means let us amass as much of it as we can. But there is such a thing (in the words of the old version) as "science falsely so called" (1 Ti 6:20); there is a wisdom that leads away

---

42   I do not mean that we should altogether abandon such things, for that would be foolish; but only that by themselves they pose no threat to the devil.

from God instead of towards him, and it becomes idolatry. Yet this world adores its own wisdom, and has no higher boast than its colossus of learning. So Omar Khayyam [43] said on his death bed -

> "O Lord, I have known you according to the sum of my ability. Pardon me, since verily my knowledge is my recommendation to you!" [44]

Mark how his knowledge was his only claim to grace; by that he commended himself to God. Yet scripture says: "God has decreed that this world will never find God by its wisdom" (1 Co 1:21); and again,

"I will crush the wisdom of the wise and the learning of the learned I will confound. Where then will you find your wise man? How will the scribe fare? Who will heed the clever debaters of this age? God has turned all the wisdom of this world into folly!" (vs. 19-20).

But as surely as we Christians think human wisdom is nonsense, so the world thinks our gospel is crazy, especially when miracles are added to it! Think how miracles of answered prayer must offend the wisdom of this world -

- miracles of healing defy the physician's wisdom, for they make curable what he reckons is incurable, and they may conquer even the grave; and

- miracles of supply defy the banker's wisdom, by creating fiscal provision that mocks the rules of their ledgers, and by making a few dollars do the work of many; and

- miracles of intervention defy the scientist's wisdom, for they mock his claim of a closed and uniform system in which divine intervention is absurd; and

- miracles of revelation defy the philosopher's wisdom, by ignoring the demands of human reason, and making the irrational the sanest knowledge in the world!

---

43   An 11th century Persian poet, but in his own time most renowned as a mathematician, philosopher, and astrologer.

44   The Ruba'iyat of Omar Khayyam, tr. by Avery & Heath-Stubbs; Penguin Classics, 1983; pg. 33.

One can hardly expect the world to be happy about its vaunted wisdom being treated so cavalierly! And since it refuses to repent, what else can the world do but wage war against any church that embraces the supernatural? But if miracles undermine the natural wisdom of this world, still more do

(ii) Miracles Strike at its Natural Pride

W. E. Henley (1849-1903), who was a cripple all his life, and suffered constant pain, wrote his poem Invictus while in hospital -

> Out of the night that covers me,
>   Black as the pit from pole to pole,
> I thank whatever gods may be
>   For my unconquerable soul.
> It matters not how straight the gate,
>   How charged with punishment the scroll,
> I am the master of my fate,
>   I am the captain of my soul. [45]

One cannot but admire his courage, for there is truly something stirring about his brave and defiant words. Certainly he showed a better character than some timorous and complaining Christians have displayed. But we cannot help, either, hearing the words of the psalmist-

> *"God sits enthroned in heaven and laughs at them; the Lord holds them in derision!" (2:4).*

How can any man be truly "master of his fate" and "captain of his soul" when every man and woman lies under sentence of death, after which comes the judgment of God? (He 9:27).

Yet the world insists upon asserting its independence from God and rejecting all claims of miracles. Why? Because each miracle shows decisively that man is not what he supposes himself to be, the master of his world. On the contrary, every time a miracle occurs in the church, notice is given that God may whenever he pleases intervene in human affairs; he can destroy the natural equilibrium, disrupt the flow of history, and take irresistible control over the whole earth. But that is intolerable! So the world keeps on pressing the church to purchase respectability at the cost of the supernatural. Would you like to live at

---

45   First and last of four stanzas.

peace with the world? Then just oblige the church to function within the parameters of human wisdom, just accept the natural limits of power. The church will then soon gain a good reputation in the councils of those who pronounce themselves wise!

Sadly, there was a time when Paul himself yielded to that pressure. Which brings us to -

PAUL AT ATHENS

1. PAUL THE PLAUSIBLE

Notice again Paul's strange confession (1 Co 2:1,3). How much out of character those words seem! Some have suggested he was merely displaying humility and Christian grace; they deny that he was actually anxious and trembling. But the same phrase is used elsewhere with an obviously literal meaning; why then should it be denied here? [46]

What happened? What stripped the great apostle of his usual aggressive confidence (which he had to re-assert against some in Corinth who judged him by the first time they met him, 2 Co 10:9,10)? What emaciated his strength?

Note that Paul came to Corinth from Athens (Ac 18:1). Perhaps, then, something had gone wrong in Athens? Luke tells us that Paul did nothing in Athens except preach one sermon on Mars Hill, the place of public assembly and debate (Ac 17:22 ff). Impressed by the cultured and highly sophisticated audience facing him, the apostle decided this was no place for the old-time gospel accompanied by miracles. He drew on all his academic learning, employed all the arts of Greek oratory, and preached a sparkling and shrewd sermon. It was in fact a marvellous

---

46 The phrase usually occurs against a background of possible punishment. So in 2 Co 7:15 the people were anxious that Titus was coming to rebuke them; and in Ep 6:5, slaves trembled before the anger of their masters; and in Ph 2:12 there is a threat of divine wrath if we neglect the salvation that has been given to us. So I take it that in 1 Co 2:3 Paul was expressing a genuine anguish of spirit, a dread of failing in Corinth to fulfil his apostolic commission, as he had apparently failed to do in Athens. Happily, his fears proved to be groundless. He preached Christ in Corinth with all the attending power of the Spirit (1 Co 1:6,7; and see also 2 :12-13, in which his preaching is placed in a charismatic setting that almost certainly refers to glossolalia).

piece of work, a masterpiece of the orator's craft, which has since then been cited in countless texts on public speaking. There was only one thing wrong: it failed! (vs. 32-34). They laughed at him! Paul knew in his heart that he was at fault. He had been called by God to do much more than preach a clever sermon and win a handful of converts (cp. Ac 22:16-18; Mk 16:15-20). Humbled, heartbroken, he quickly left Athens, never to return!

But while he was walking between Athens and Corinth (perhaps 60km) God dealt with him, and he arrived at Corinth as ...

2. PAUL THE POWERFUL

He was a changed man. He had made certain irrevocable decisions -

"When I first came among you, my friends, and began to preach about the truth of God, I resolved to abandon any pretence of eloquence or wisdom. I was determined that among you I would know nothing except Jesus Christ, and him crucified. I actually arrived in Corinth void of strength, filled with anxiety, trembling with dread. The message I preached, the truth I proclaimed, were not clothed with clever plausibility, but came with a demonstration of the power of the Holy Spirit. I wanted your faith to stand, not on human wisdom, but on the power of God" (1 Co 2:4-5.

What Paul had failed to do in Athens he did surpassingly well in Corinth: he raised up a great church, in which, if anything, there were too many miracles! Writing to them later he said that "they lacked not one of the charismata" (1 Co 1:7). Yet, though his first visit among them had lasted for nearly two years (so he had had ample time to instruct them in the use of the gifts of the Spirit), when he wrote to them he had to calm down their commitment to the supernatural! (12:1 ff.) Apparently during that first visit to Corinth he was so chagrined by the Athenian experience that he could not bring himself to hinder in any way the flow of miracles!

CONCLUSION

Note that something was irretrievably lost at Athens. Corinth was an important city, but it could never exert the influence of Athens, which was the cultural heart of the ancient world. As Athens went, so went the world. Had Paul created in Athens the church he built at Corinth, its influence would have been enormous.

But the opportunity was lost and could not be regained, or at least, not by Paul. He never visited Athens again.

The lesson is clear: any time the church buys respectability or worldly acceptance at the cost of the supernatural it must pay a terrible price. As often as the church assembles in worship something should happen that only God can do! (1 Co 14:24-26)

I do not mean that miracles by themselves are sufficient. Christ must also be preached, and preached fully, and without such preaching miracles mean nothing. Satan can easily produce his own counterfeit signs and wonders (Mt 7:21-23; 2 Th 2:9; etc.). [47] But equally, without the demonstration of the Spirit, the gospel may become just one among many competing religious and secular philosophies. The true pattern was declared by Paul: not word alone, nor work alone; but rather, "fully preach" the gospel by both word and work - that is, sermon and sign, preaching and power, message and miracle must always go hand in hand.

We value all natural skills and resources, and should make full use of them; [48] but we dare not depend upon them alone, for we Christians are always called to live in a dimension beyond ourselves (2 Co 3:18).

"Athens" or "Corinth" - Natural Wisdom or Pentecostal power - the worst or the best. That is always the choice facing the church. Which will you choose?

---

47 Nearly all the various phenomena that occur in Christian circles may happen just as readily in a heathen environment. They are in the main part of the common coin of human religious experience. No miracle is worth anything unless it occurs within a context (1) of sound theology; and (2) of divine love.

48 Notice that Paul, despite his passionate words in 1 Co 2:1-5, still wrote a brilliant letter to the Corinthians, employing many persuasive arts, and powerful writing techniques. The same letter also contains Paul's magnificent ode in praise of love (ch. 13), one of the most exquisite paeans ever to flow from a human pen. So Paul did continue to use "clever and persuasive" words, and much wisdom and shrewd appeal in his letters. But he had learned absolutely to keep such things subsidiary to the power of God.

CHAPTER SEVEN:

PYJAMA CORDS?

I was at church with my wife one Sunday morning, many years ago, when out came the preacher, onto the platform, and up to the pulpit, with a pajama cord hanging over the belt of his trousers. Plainly he had slept in that day, then found he had no time to dress properly. So he had simply pulled his trousers on over his pyjamas, along with a shirt and tie, and rushed off to church. That dangling cord gripped the eye. The sermon was hopelessly outclassed. That swinging tassel exerted a fascination that could not be denied.

There are various cousins of that pyjama cord, which trouble the wider church. I mean preacherly foibles and follies that distract attention from the gospel and hinder the effectiveness of the pulpit.

MONEY-SEEKERS

Eusebius (7:30) tells the story of a bishop of Antioch during the latter part of the 3rd century, whose name was Paul of Samosata. He was a marvelous orator, who succeeded, despite humble origins, in amassing vast wealth from his preaching. Bishop Paul loved pomp and splendour; he craved adulation. So he was delighted when crowds thronged to hear him and tumultuously applauded his sermons. Wherever he went, he organized choirs of lovely young women to travel with him, who cast flower petals before him, waved banners over his head, and sang at his meetings. When he was at the pulpit he furiously denounced other preachers, and was always surrounded by bodyguards. He eventually fell into heresy, was denounced, defrocked, and banished.

He sounds much like some preachers of the 20th century! For we too have suffered the misfortune in our time of a cluster of preachers who have used the pulpit to get rich.

Among the various wealth-gatherers are some who promise that anyone who speaks the right kind of words can change anything in this world and get anything they want. That problem too is an old one, as the ancient Greek playwright Aristophanes showed in his play The Clouds. Strepsiades is speaking to his son Pheidippides -

> Strep. . . . look this way.
> See you that wicket, and the lodge beyond?
>
> Phei. I see, and prithee, what is that, my father?
>
> Strep. That is the thinking-house of sapient souls.
> There dwell the men who teach - aye, who persuade us -
> That heaven is one vast fire-extinguisher
> Placed round about us, and that we're the cinders.
> Aye, and they'll teach (only they'll want some money),
> How one may speak and conquer, right or wrong. [49]

I hope that you, my reader, have never been muddied from that sewer.

A BAD CASE OF NERVES

Do you shake in your shoes while you wait for your turn to speak? Take heart! Some public speakers (I am among them) never overcome the distress of nervousness before they step up to the lectern, or into the pulpit. Others suffer from nerves only in unfamiliar situations. Perhaps you should be suspicious of anyone who claims to be free of nerves; the problem troubling such people may be the worse one of careless indifference.

Nervous tension should be your friend, not your enemy. Indeed, it seems to be a universal law of God that all power must come out of a state of tension. I cannot think of any power-source that does not depend upon some kind of underlying tension - lightning; an electric current; steam; hydro; tornadoes; sea waves; internal combustion; nuclear; even a human fist!

Your fluttering nerves can be, and are, an ideal source of that tension; which means that the same power that has been immobilising you can be changed into a source of boundless energy. Indeed, even if you are not nervous, you will still have to stir up the energy level that nerves would have produced.

---

49 Rogers, op. cit., pg. 156.

So don't try to fight or eradicate nerves, just use them!

Yet you need to recognize that there are two kinds of nervous tension -

1. POSITIVE

This is the kind of tension that is stimulated by a new environment or by a challenge. It makes the pulse beat faster, the adrenaline flow, and pricks every fibre into alert readiness to perform. Embrace this tension. Put it into forward gear. Use it as a source of personal empowerment. It is your ally, not an internal poison. But there is also another kind of tension -

2. NEGATIVE

This is a state of agitation arising from some feeling of inadequacy, or of unfitness for the task, or from a fear of failure because of lack of preparation.

Martin Luther, while he was still a novice in the Catholic monastery, was once given some drastic counsel on this problem by his monastic superior, Dr Staupitz -

> "Ah, my friend," Luther later said to another young and nervous preacher, " . . . I feared the pulpit perhaps as greatly as you do; yet I had to do it; I was forced to preach . . . Ah! how I feared the pulpit! . . . Under this very pear tree I advanced more than 15 arguments to Dr Staupitz (as to why I should not preach). With (those arguments) I declined my call. But they did me no good. When I finally said, `Dr Staupitz, you are taking my life; I shall not live a quarter-year,' he replied: `In God's name! Our Lord God has many things to do; he is in need of wise people in heaven too!'" [50]

IMPATIENCE

Forget those stories you have read about the young preacher who went to a town and within a year had a thousand people (or more) crowding into his church each Sunday. Yes, it does happen, but so seldom that you would be absurd to turn it into a paradigm. For most of us, preaching is patient work, with results accumulating slowly, and usually in fits and

50 What Luther Says, vol 3, pg 1110.

starts. But then, that is what the whole of life is like for most people, and they must learn patience if they would achieve anything worthwhile. But those restless souls who never stay long enough in one place to succeed reap a poor harvest.

> If they just went straight they might go far;
>   They are strong, and brave and true;
> But they're always tired of the things that are,
>   And they want the strange and new.
> They say, `Could I find my proper groove,
>   What a deep mark I would make!'
> So they chop and change, and each fresh move
>   Is only a fresh mistake. [51]

So ignore the exceptions (unless you happen to be one). The ordinary rule of life is that the way to win is through quiet, steady, persevering, patient toil (Ro 2:6-7).

BAD HABITS

Here are some appropriate quotes on the need to watch for, and eradicate, the various nervous habits that over the years have undone some of the most gifted speakers. Keep a look out for these in your own ministry. Admonish your spouse, or some trusted friend, to be merciless in drawing your attention to any such irritating behaviour if you begin to fall into it.

1. NERVOUS HABITS

(a) MARTIN LUTHER

"A preacher should have the following qualifications:

1. Ability to teach.
2. A good mind.
3. Eloquence.
4. A good voice.
5. A good memory.
6. Power to leave off.
7. Diligence.

---

51 Robert Service, "The Men That Don't Fit In", st. 2; The Best of Robert Service, Dodd, Mead, & Co, New York, 1953.

8.   Whole-souled devotion to his calling.
9.   Willingness to be bothered by everyone.
10. Patience to bear all things.

> "In ministers nothing is seen more easily or more
> quickly than their faults. A preacher may have a
> hundred virtues, yet they may all be obscured by a single
> defect, the world is now so bad. Dr Jonas has all the
> attributes of a good preacher, but people cannot forgive
> the good man for hawking and spitting so often." [52]

(b) RICHARD CORBET

This worthy bishop of Oxford in the early 17th cent was also known as a
poet and wit. But the stress of one occasion became too great for him.
He had to preach before King James I, but found himself unable to rise to
the challenge, and destroyed the effect of his oratory by nervous fiddling.

Someone, who perhaps had been a victim of the cleric's sharp tongue,
composed these mocking lines to commemorate the fiasco -

> A reverend dean
> With his ruff starched clean,
>   Did preach before the king;
> In his band-string was spied
> A ring that was tied,
>   Was that not a pretty thing?
>
> The ring without doubt
> Was the thing put him out,
>   So oft he forgot what was next;
> For all that were there,
> On my conscience, dare swear
>   That he handled it more than his text! [53]

52   Luther, quoted by Kepler, op. cit.
53   John Aubrey (1626-97), Brief Lives; Folio Society, London, 1975; pg. 88.

(c) LEWIS CARROLL

Said the Queen to Alice,

"Look up, speak nicely, and don't twiddle your fingers all the time." [54]

How annoying all such mannerisms of speech or habits of behavior can become. Yet the problem is widespread, and certainly not restricted to the Christian pulpit, as we learn from::

(d) SEI SHONAGON

Miss Shonagon was a lady-in-waiting to the empress in the royal court of Japan in the 10th century. She wrote a charming Pillow Book, full of delightful lists of observations about human behaviour. One of her lists is called "Different Ways of Speaking", and contains only three items:

- priest's language.

- The speech of men and women.

- Common people always tend to add extra syllables to their words. [55]

I know just what she was talking about! "Priest's language" and "extra syllables" abound in Christian pulpits too. You should shun like a pestilence such speech mannerisms and repetitions as:

- "you know", and other superfluous words constantly interpolated into your speech

- the kind of Pentecostal profanity that consists of mindless fill-ins like "glory", "praise the Lord", "hallelujah"

- vacuous mumblings like "er . . . ah . . . um . . . "

- repeated and meaningless interjections like "see? alright! . . . O.K.?"

- absurdly useless and pretentious extra syllables, like "Lord-

---

54   Through the Looking Glass, Ch. 2.
55   Tr. by Ivan Morris; Penguin Classics, 1967; pg. 25.

ah . . . God-ah . . . Christ-ah").

Tremble at the thought of endless repetitions of "yea" (when praying aloud, or prophesying); and any such verbal oddity.

Sometimes speakers use these devices in the mistaken idea that they add dramatic effect to their words. They don't. They are merely tedious, aggravating, and distracting.

Would you shrink from handling a viper? So you should recoil from using any kind of "priest's language" (as Sei Shonagon called it) - that is, adopting a "pious" intonation, a "religious" manner - the moment you get behind a pulpit. There is no reason to speak in anything other than your ordinary voice (albeit more vigorously than usual), or to use words in anything other than a normal way.

I once heard a prayer that went something like this:

> "Father God, hear us Father God, when we pray Father God to you Father God. Father God you know Father God that Father God we can do nothing Father God without your help Father God. So stand with us Father God in all your strength Father God and stretch out Father God your mighty hand to work miracles Father God among your people, Father God, etc. etc."

How ridiculous! How irksome! Yet how often one hears that kind of thing!

Guard also against developing such mannerisms as:

- constantly pulling at an ear
- frequently rubbing your nose or your forehead
- moving nervously around, backwards and forwards, from side to side
- pulling a handkerchief in and out, in and out
- putting your hands into your pockets, and out, and in
- endlessly removing and replacing your spectacles
- continually hitching up your garments; doing up and

undoing a button

- fixing either a smile or a frown upon your face, no matter what subject is being dealt with

- never looking the people in the eye; always staring upward, or gazing upon the wall or a window, or looking over their heads

- tugging at your garments; folding and unfolding your hands; shifting them from your front to your back over and over again.

All such repeated patterns of speech or action become distracting; people cannot help but notice them and become ever more fascinated (or irritated) by them, to the detriment of your message.

It is a sad reflection that after a thousand years (since Sei Shonagon noticed the mannerisms of her Buddhist monks), the same follies can still be observed in our churches. So we still suffer under preachers who adopt a sort of holy sing-song, or lift their voices two or three tones above normal, or in some other way assume an artificial style as soon as they begin to speak. They mark themselves as "common", along with those who allow themselves to fall into any kind of vexing habit.

2. LONG SERMONS

"It is commonly said these are the three qualifications that mark a good preacher: first, that he step up; second, that he speak up, and say something worthwhile; third, that he know when to stop ... To preach long is no art; but to preach and to teach right well, that is work, that is labor!" [56] ... "To me a long sermon is an abomination, for the desire of the audience to listen is destroyed, and the preacher only defeats himself. On this account I took Dr Bugenhagen severely to task, for although he preaches long sermons with spontaneity and pleasure, nevertheless it is a mistake." [57]

---

56   What Luther Says, vol 3, pg 1110.
57   Kepler, op. cit.

There is no special virtue in length. Luther's sermons (not his lectures) seldom exceeded 30 minutes; Robert Schuller too keeps to half an hour; even Spurgeon stayed within an hour. More humble preachers would be wiser to say two or three worthwhile things in less than 30 minutes, than to punish the people with a 60-minute mash of mind-numbing repetitions.

When Alice was on trial, the White Rabbit asked the King,

> "Where shall I begin, please your Majesty?"

> "Begin at the beginning," the king said very gravely, "and go on till you come to the end: then stop." [58]

Good advice for any preacher. If you are under a cultural obligation to speak for forty minutes or more, make sure you put in the requisite study (one great preacher reckoned he needed an hour of study for every minute of sermon!)

Remember also: you are more likely to receive divine guidance at home in your study, free from distractions, than you are at the pulpit. Give yourself more study time and you won't need so much pulpit time. Seldom do I hear a sermon that has enough content truly to need, or deserve, forty-five minutes. Mostly, when all the empty repetitions, superfluous verbiage, mindless syllables ("er, ah, yes, you know"), and the like, are removed, the whole thing could have been said better in twenty minutes!

3. RAMBLING SERMONS

Luther, on a famous preacher's tendency to wander from his text, said this:

> "Bugenhagen says whatever occurs to him. Jonas used to say, 'Don't hail every soldier you meet.' That is right. Bugenhagen often takes along everyone whom he meets with him. Let him take care to keep to the text and attend to what is before him and make people understand that. Those preachers who say whatever comes into their mouths remind me of a maid going to market. When she meets another maid she stops and chats a

---

58   Lewis Carroll, Alice in Wonderland, Ch. 13.

while, then she meets another and talks with her, too, and then a third and a fourth, and so gets to market very slowly. So with preachers who wander off the text; they would like to say everything at one time, but they can't...

"When Morlin, Medler, or Jacob preaches, it is just as when the plug is drawn from a full cask; the liquid runs out as long as there is any left within. But such volubility of tongue doesn't really lay hold of the audience, though it delights some, nor is it even instructive. It is better to speak distinctly, so that what is said may be comprehended." [59]

CONCLUSION

Alexander the Great regarded the Greek hero Achilles as happy because he had such a herald as Homer to sing his valour. Once, when a messenger approached him, showing signs of great joy in his expression, Alexander cried: "What are you going to announce to me that is worthy of such happiness, unless perhaps Homer has come back to life?" [60]

The hero and the herald came together well in Achilles and Homer. How about you and Christ? Has the Master reason to be happy because you are his herald; or should he rather blush with disappointment?

---

59 Kepler, op. cit.
60 I have lost the source of this anecdote. Perhaps I found it in Arrian, or Quintus Curtius.

CHAPTER EIGHT:

PANGS OF DISAPPOINTMENT

Disappointment is a dark thread woven through the lives of most pastors and preachers. If you have felt, or still feel, its fierce stab, be comforted by realizing you are not alone. St Augustine once found it necessary to encourage a gifted speaker who nonetheless had become frustrated by apparent failure -

"You have made confession and complaint that it has often befallen you that in the course of a lengthened and languid address you have become profitless and distasteful even to yourself, not to speak of the learner whom you have been endeavouring to instruct by your utterance, and the other parties who have been present as hearers . . .

"One thing which I have heard you make the subject of your complaint above all others, is the fact that your discourse seemed to yourself to be poor and spiritless when you were instructing any one in the Christian name. . .

"Indeed, with me, too, it is almost always the fact that my speech displeases myself. For I am covetous of something better, the possession of which I frequently enjoy within me before I commence to body it forth in intelligible words; and then when my capacities of expression prove inferior to my inner apprehensions, I grieve over the inability which my tongue has betrayed in answering to my heart. For it is my wish that he who hears me should have the same complete understanding of the subject which I have myself; and I perceive that I fail to speak in a manner calculated to effect that . . . " [61]

---

61   Post-Nicene Fathers, vol 3, pg 283,292,284.

On another cause of frustration, Augustine wrote -

> "A sense of weariness is also induced upon the speaker when he has a hearer who remains unmoved, either in that he is actually not stirred by any feeling, or in that he does not indicate by any motion of the body that he understands or that he is pleased with what is said. Not that it is a becoming disposition in us to be greedy of the praises of men, but that the things which we minister are of God; and the more we love those to whom we discourse, the more desirous we are that they should be pleased with the matters which are held forth for their salvation: so that if we do not succeed in this, we are pained, and we are weakened, and become broken-spirited in the midst of our course, as if we were wasting our efforts to no purpose." [62]

> Unconsciously echoing St Augustine's disappointment that he could never put into words exactly what he felt in his spirit, the renowned 19th cent. Scottish author, Thomas Carlyle, wrote -

> "Men's words are a poor exponent of their thought; nay, their thought itself is a poor exponent of the inward unnamed Mystery, wherefrom both thought and action have their birth. No man can explain himself, can get himself explained; men see not one another, but distorted phantasms which they call one another; which they hate and go to battle with: for all battle is well said to be misunderstanding." [63]

EXPECT TO BE MISUNDERSTOOD

If you preach, you will be misunderstood; no one, in fact, will **ever** understand your words as you intended them to be heard; and you may expect frequently to be thoroughly misunderstood, to be accused of saying, or at least of meaning, things that never so much as entered your mind!

---

62   Ibid, pg 293.
63   The French Revolution, Bk Three, Ch. Two.

If you cannot cope with such distresses graciously, winsomely, and patiently, then abandon the pulpit at once!

But I hope that instead you will resolve neither to be deterred nor discouraged by failure, whether real or imagined! The world will still be the same tomorrow morning, with the sun shining just as brightly, and the birds singing just as merrily. If you choose to weep, you will weep alone -

> Laugh, and the world laughs with you;
>   Weep, and you weep alone;
> For the sad old earth must borrow its mirth,
>   But has trouble enough of its own.
> Sing, and the hills will answer;
>   Sigh, it is lost on the air;
> The echoes bound to a joyful sound,
>   But shrink from voicing care. [64]

The same idea was expressed more seriously by the 19th century novelist Thomas Hardy, in his story about a young woman who had been seduced by a wealthy landowner. Because a child was born of the illicit union, she hid herself away for a long time; but then she wearied of isolation and determined to venture forth -

> "A resolution which had surprised herself had brought her into the fields for the first time in many months. After wearing and wasting her palpitating heart with every engine of regret that lonely inexperience could devise, common sense had illumined her. She felt that she would do well to be useful again - to taste anew sweet independence at any price. The past was past; whatever it had been was no more at hand. Whatever its consequences, time would close over them; they would all in a few years be as if they had never been, and she herself grassed down and forgotten. Meanwhile the trees were just as green as before; the birds sang and the sun shone as clearly now as ever. The familiar surroundings had not darkened because of her grief, nor sickened because of her pain.

---

64   Solitude St. One; Ella Wheeler Wilcox (1850-1919).

"She might have seen that what had bowed her head so profoundly - the thought of the world's concern at her situation - was founded on an illusion. She was not an existence, an experience, a passion, a structure of sensations, to anybody but herself. To all humankind besides Tess was only a passing thought. Even to friends she was no more than a frequently passing thought." [65]

Are any of us in better case? Your best sermon will be as soon forgotten as your worst, and in neither case will there be much change in the world! So you might as well throw off your gloom, chuckle, and get on with life.

EXTEMPORANEOUS?

To use notes or not to use them, that is the question! On this matter it is impossible to generalize. Some great preachers have written their sermons out in full, and then read them from the pulpit. "A read sermon," as someone has said, "is not necessarily a dead sermon."

At the other extreme have been magnificent pulpiteers who memorized their sermons, and entered the pulpit without even a scrap of notes. Then many successful homileticians (probably the majority) have used the kind of skeleton outlines that are given as examples below. Others have extemporized, going into the pulpit with hardly more than a text and an idea or two. My own constant practice has been to prepare skeleton outlines, which seldom exceed the two sides of a piece of notepaper. I am generally content to approach the pulpit with little more than the main headings and sub-headings of my message, which I have in any case usually committed to memory - although I like to have the notes there, just in case!

Each preacher must find his or her own most comfortable practice. Do what best suits your own personality, temperament, gifts, and, above all, what will best enable you to declare the Word of Life to your hearers.

But no matter what style you adopt, one thing is required of all: the utmost preparation. True, it is possible to prepare magnificently, and yet find a sermon fail miserably; and equally possible to stumble wearily

65   Tess of the D'Urbervilles Part Two, Ch. 14.

into the pulpit ill-prepared and ill-humoured, and yet make a stunning impact upon a congregation. But that does not excuse wilful slovenliness. To the extent that time and opportunity allow, every preacher should labour diligently to prepare the best possible sermons in the best possible way. There is no higher office in the nation than that of the pulpit. It deserves our uttermost efforts, our highest sacrifices, our most eager dedication.

As Sirach said long ago -

> If you want people to listen to you, then prepare well what you want to say. Gather together all the learning you can, and then speak up! But the heart of a fool spins like a cart wheel, and his thoughts go round and round like an axle" (33:4-5).

I regret that I have heard more than enough foolish sermons that spin around and go nowhere, preached by preachers too lazy to "prepare well".

BUILDING A TREASURE CHEST

Wisdom should be gleaned from all possible sources. The notable Sirach drew upon an extensive education, and upon his far-flung travels (which in those days, 200 B.C., would have been both exhausting and perilous). He wrote -

> "A good education will bring you knowledge of many things, and those who have a wide experience know what they are talking about. How little an inexperienced person knows! But someone who has traveled far becomes wise and clever. During my own travels I have experienced many things, and I have learned much more than I will ever put into words. Indeed, I have often confronted death, but the things I have learned enabled me to escape safely" (34:9-13).

That same learning and experience, even if you never leave your study, is available to anyone who spends enough time reading, studying, thinking, digesting - not just sacred literature, but across the whole span of writing: poetry, fiction, art, physics, astronomy, history, geography, music - indeed, whatever expresses the deepest feelings and achievements of the human spirit, whatever will bring the preacher closer to all that it means to be human.

Even music, listened to well, can deepen the soul's sensitivities -

> "Is it any weakness, pray, to be wrought on by exquisite music? - to feel its wondrous harmonies searching the subtlest windings of your soul, the delicate fibres of life where no memory can penetrate, and binding together your whole being past and present in one unspeakable vibration: melting you in one moment with all the tenderness, all the love that has been scattered through the toilsome years, concentrating in one emotion of heroic courage or resignation all the hard-learnt lessons of self-renouncing sympathy, blending your present joy with past sorrow, and your present sorrow with all your past joy? [66]

Let us admit then that style and skill do enhance power. I do not mean that you should try to be clever - especially the kind of cleverness that draws attention to itself rather than to Christ, or to the Word. Yet there is no credit in doing a job poorly that we have skill to do well. Every preacher should exert every effort to excel to the limit of his or her ability, for to do otherwise is to scorn the gifts of God.

EMOTION

As later notes will show, there will always be plenty of room for emotion, both in preaching of the Word and in response to it. A good sermon must appeal to the heart as well as to the mind. But emotion in church is a thing to be handled with care, for it may easily turn the minds of the people away from genuine faith and onto spurious feeling -

> "Dr Martin Lloyd-Jones [67] believed that, while the truth ought to result in profound emotion, the cultivation of `emotionalism' was thoroughly alien to true Christianity. Feeling alone (by itself) he saw as not merely valueless, it was positively dangerous. Emotionalism is ever the most real, because the most subtle, enemy of

---

66   George Eliot (1819-80), Adam Bede, ch. 33.
67   A renowned British preacher, author, and theologian.

evangelicalism. True feeling must be the result of truth believed and understood, and he frequently gave warning against the type of service where attempts are made to induce emotion by working up the meeting with music and choruses, or by the telling of moving stories. `Tears are a poor criterion for faith; being carried away in a meeting by eloquence or singing or excitement is not the same as committing oneself to Christ. To aim at emotion is the surest way to produce counterfeit Christians.'

"Thus his belief was that in a service where feeling could be restrained it ought to be restrained. The power of God was more likely to be known in a solemn stillness than amid noise and excitement." [68]

BLUNDERS

According to Sir Thomas Malory, among the Knights of the Round table Sir Tristram was second only to Sir Lancelot in prowess and virtue. Nonetheless, on a certain day he was defeated in a tournament, thrown off his horse, "and was wroth out of measure and sorely ashamed of that fall." But one of his friends approached him and said,

"Lo, Sir Tristram, here may a man prove old sayings: be a man never so good, he may have a fall; and he was never so wise but he might be mistaken; and he rideth well who never fell." [69]

Nothing is more certain than you will commit some ghastly blunder when you least expect to do so. No preacher can avoid the occasional loss of control over the sermon, or over the way it is delivered. Some unconscious lapse from good taste, some unwitting indiscretion, some unfortunate bungling of words, some stumbling fall, can overtake the best of preachers. What the French would call a faux pas is slyly waiting to snare the most cautious speaker.

68   Dr Martin Lloyd-Jones: The First 40 Years, by Iaian H. Murray; Banner of Truth Trust, Edinburgh; pg. 216.
69   Le Morte d'Arthur (1469); ed. R. M. Lumiansky; Collier MacMillan, London, 1986; pg. 315.

What should you do when in the full flight of oratory you realize you have just cried out, "Pharaoh and all his Pharisees came pounding across the desert"? How do you cope with seeing an entire congregation dissolve into embarrassed giggles, yet you have no idea what you said to amuse them?

William H. Willimon tells about the pastor who was angered by the immodest attire of some of his female parishioners. He decided to address the matter in a sermon, and told how he saw a young lady coming into the church dressed in a pair of skimpy and tight-fitting shorts. He cried, "I determined to do something about it. It was my duty as a pastor. I confronted her and asked her to come down to my study and talk about it. I shared scripture with her and told her how those shorts looked. And I'll tell you, in 15 minutes I had those shorts off of her!"

Dr Willimon comments: "He tried desperately to win back the hysterically laughing congregation, but he tried in vain. Each time he attempted to go on with his sermon some corner of the congregation would erupt into renewed laughter." [70]

CUT YOUR LOSSES

There have been two or three occasions in my own ministry when nothing was left except to bring the meeting to as quick an end as was decently possible. Either I or someone else had committed some awful blooper, and it was hopeless to suppose the congregation could be brought back to a state of reverence.

Probably the worst thing you can do is try to retrace your steps, and start again. You would do better to cut your losses and vanish as swiftly as you decently can!

Pierre Nicole, a 17th century French mathematician and ethicist, once attended a fashionable Parisian function, and resolved at the end of it to express his personal thanks to the hostess. He took her aside and effusively declared his gratitude for the honour she had shown him, and at the end of a long parade of compliments "assured her that her 'lovely little' eyes had totally enchanted him." He left the party feeling satisfied

---

70   From an article, "Sermon Slips", in The Christian Ministry journal, Nov-
      Dec 1988; pg. 39.

that he had done the right thing, only to be told by a friend that to call a lady's eyes "little" was a terrible faux pas, and that she must certainly be deeply offended. Filled with shame, Nicole ran back to the party, approached the hostess again, begged her pardon, then tried to undo his error by a different array of compliments. He enthusiastically declared that "he had never seen such large eyes, large lips, large hands, or such a generally large person altogether, in his whole life." He left behind him a stunned and dismayed audience.

When you have made a mistake, you should either ignore it, or make a brief correction, or join the congregation in its laughter against you. One thing you assuredly should not do is stand there stricken with embarrassment, metaphorically wringing your hands in despair. Nor is it ever excusable to break out in anger against the people, as if the fault were theirs.

CONCLUSION

"Contentment united with godliness," said Paul, "is great gain." Preachers are sometimes prone to apply those words to everyone but themselves. They claim a special dispensation from God to be frustrated, disappointed, restless, anxious, driven, ever craving more and more. Could there be a more foolish frame in which to build a life? Henry Howard, the Earl of Surrey (1517-47), expressed Paul's sentiment in poetry -

> Martial, the things that do attain
> The happy life be these, I find:
> The riches left, not got with pain;
> The fruitful ground, the quiet mind:
>
> The equal friend, no grudge nor strife;
> No charge of rule nor governance;
> Without disease, the healthful life;
> The household of continuance:
>
> The mean diet, no delicate fare;
> True wisdom join'd with simpleness;
> The night dischargèd of all care,
> Where wine the wit may not oppress:

The faithful wife, without debate;
Such sleeps as may beguile the night:
Contented with thine own estate,
we wish for death, ne fear his might. [71]

---

71 The Happy Life. Martial (circa 40-104) was a Roman poet and
epigrammist, and the earl's poem is based on translations of his aphorisms.

CHAPTER NINE:

STAIRWAYS TO THE STARS

Every sermon should open a doorway to heaven. That should be true whether or not the preacher is highly skilled, for just the same task is laid upon those who possess only average abilities as upon those who are innately gifted.

One of the most magnificent works of art in the world is the pair of extraordinary bronze doors to the baptistery [72] in Florence that Lorenzo Ghiberti created during the first 40 years of the 15th century. "The mingled grace and grandeur of these compositions," says one writer, "is beyond all praise. Ghiberti is undoubtedly one of the most accomplished workers in metal that has ever lived." Michelangelo called them the "Gates of Paradise"! Georgio Vasari describes them thus -

> "Every single detail of Lorenzo's doors demonstrates what the skill and genius of an accomplished sculptor can effect when he is casting figures in the round, in half relief, in low relief, or very low relief. In the imaginative composition, the striking poses of his male and female figures, the perspectives, and the consistently graceful bearing of both sexes, Lorenzo demonstrated his perfect grasp of decorum, expressing gravity in the old and lightness and grace in the young. The doors are undeniably perfect in every way and must rank as the finest masterpiece ever created, in either ancient or modern times. It would be difficult to praise Lorenzo too much, seeing that one day Michelangelo Buonarroti himself, standing to look at the doors and being asked what he thought of them and whether they were not beautiful remarked, 'They are so beautiful that they would grace the entrance to Paradise.'

---

72 In the Roman Catholic church prior to the 16th century, a separate church building in which the rite of baptism was practised.

"This tribute was indeed fitting, and it was offered by a man in a position to judge. And Lorenzo well deserved to bring the doors to completion, having started them when he was twenty and slaved on them for over forty years. . . . Among the many verses both in Latin and Italian which have been written at various times to commemorate Lorenzo I shall, to avoid troubling the reader further, content myself with quoting this:

> When Michelangelo the panels saw
> Gleaming upon the church in gilded bronze
> Amaz'd he stood; after long wonder thus
> The solemn silence broke: `O work divine!
> O door worthy of Heaven!' [73]

Splendid as Lorenzo's "Gates of Paradise" may be, the humblest preacher whose words carry his or her hearers to the throne of God has wrought more finely; long after the bronze doors have crumbled into dust each godly word will continue to sparkle like diamonds in the heavenlies.

How to craft sermons that are "Gateways to Paradise" is now our theme.

EFFECTIVE COMMUNICATION

There are five parts to good communication -

1. THE MORAL

Nothing can replace the good character of the speaker, who must be without guile, genuine and sincere. This is always the most convincing part of the argument. The truism is nonetheless true: actions speak louder than words. No matter how loudly you raise your voice, your behaviour will speak more loudly, and to greater effect. But we are sometimes prone to the same reaction Ralph Waldo Emerson [74] felt, when he said,

"The louder he talked of his honour, the faster we counted our spoons."

Even children learnt the lesson in the ancient nursery rhyme,

> A man of words but not of deeds

---

73   Op. cit. Vol. One; pg. 116, 117, 120.
74   1803-82. American poet and essayist.

Is like a garden full of weeds.

Even more ancient, and more apposite, are some words of St Jerome, [75] which first gave rise to the saying, "Practise what you preach." They are found in a letter [76] the great teacher wrote to a young man, Nepotian, who had abandoned a promising military career to go into the Christian ministry. The letter presents a systematic treatise on the duties of a pastor, and on the life-style and character a man of God should display. Jerome's stern demand for holiness, integrity, purity, humility, and simplicity in a pastor, void of ostentation, pomp, and all love of riches, aroused against him much fierce indignation. [77] Yet his counsel was in general wise, and in one place he said -

> "Read the divine scriptures constantly; never, indeed, let the sacred volume be out of your hand. What you have to teach, you must first learn yourself. ... Do not let your actions turn your words into a lie, lest when you speak in church someone may mentally reply: 'Why do you not practise what you preach?'" [78]

Then a thousand years before Jerome, the Chinese philosopher Confucius gave this counsel to his disciples -

> "(The superior man) acts before he speaks, and afterwards speaks according to his actions. ... The superior man is modest in his speech, but exceeds in his actions." [79]

Not all the world's most beautiful sentiments, no matter how nobly expressed, can undo the discordant screech of contrary deeds. I will

---

75   Circa 342-420, scholar, writer, teacher, he has been called "the most learned and eloquent of the Latin Fathers.

76   Letter #52, written in 394 A.D. Quoted from The Nicene and Post-Nicene Fathers, Second Series, Vol. Six; Eerdmans Pub. Co., 1979 reprint of the original volume of 1892; pg. 93.

77   Which he apparently anticipated: "You have compelled me, my dear Nepotian, ... once more to open my mouth ... and to expose myself to the stabs of every tongue. For I could escape from criticism by writing nothing ... and I knew when I took up my pen that the shafts of all gainsayers would be launched against me!" (Ibid., Section # 17)

78   Section #7.

79   The Confucian Analects, 2:13; 14:29.

know what you truly think, not merely when I hear your words, but when I observe your behaviour.

2. THE ETHICAL

No one can wholly meet the demands placed before a pastor; but as far as your strength will stretch you should strive to be competent in your task, accurate in your information, qualified for the role you have assumed. To do less is to play the hypocrite. Do not pretend to be what you are not, but let true authority rise out of the people sensing that you are in fact more than you claim. In another letter [80] Jerome scorns the expedient, but unethical philosophy, "the end justifies the means." He is dealing in particular with his manner of conducting a debate, and insists that he uses only fair arguments, disdaining deceit or bullying tactics -

> "I might have used such arguments if I had wanted victory so much that I became willing to make use even of things that are contrary to the principles of scripture. I could have taken the line - so often employed by strong men in controversy - of justifying the means by the end."

But he declined to do so. No matter how desirable the end, he preferred not to reach it rather than employ unethical means. The same rule should still prevail in the church.

3. THE RATIONAL

The first appeal of the preacher must be to the mind, reaching for conviction of the truth. This requires that we ourselves think clearly, and present our message logically, forcefully, and convincingly.

4. THE EMOTIONAL

Though we eschew the burden of having to persuade people to yield to our message, nonetheless, we must reach into their hearts, hoping to stir their emotions as well as their minds. We cannot help but strive for a response. The final responsibility may not be ours, since it belongs only to the Holy Spirit, but no real preacher can be content never to see to see men and women yielding to the claims of Christ. We have been told, after all, to go into the world and "make disciples", not just occupy a pulpit. We want more, much more than an audience, but a congregation

---

80   Letter #48, written in 393, to his friend Pammachius.

of saints, people who are living in a covenanted relationship with each other under the lordship of Christ. Our major appeal must be to their minds; but we will never achieve our goal unless we also warm their hearts.

> "The dying words of the German poet Goethe were, 'Light, light, let there be more light.' When the 20th-century Spanish philosopher Miguel de Unamuno reflected on those words, he said, 'It is not more light we need, but more warmth! We die of cold, not of darkness. It is not the night that kills, but the frost!' " [81]

5. THE PRACTICAL

> There was a young belle of old Natchez
> Whose garments were always in patches;
> When comment arose
> On the state of her clothes,
> She drawled, When Ah itchez, Ah scratchez! [82]

When someone asks you to scratch his back, there is little use in rubbing his hand. Without compromising our duty to preach the "whole counsel of God", [83] we must nonetheless strive to apply the healing balm of scripture to an actual wound. Scratch people where they are itching. Bandage what is diseased, not what is well. Fill up the empty bucket, not the full one. Write on the blank page, not the one that is already crowded. If your message is not relevant to your hearers then you will hardly hold their interest.

I suppose one of the worst sins a preacher can commit is to bore the audience, which you will certainly do if they see no possible use or benefit to them in what you say. God forbid that your hearers should ever react as his companions once did to a droning Monk. He had just spun them a gloomy tale, or rather, preached a dreary sermon, which was

---

81   Quoted by Anthony B. Robinson, in an article in the Christian Century, Nov 3, 1993.
82   One of the limericks of the American humorous writer Ogden Nash (1902-71).
83   See the next heading, just below.

quite out of character with the environment, and far away from the present need or interest of the listeners -

> "'Ho, my good sir, no more!' exclaimed the Knight;
> 'What you have said so far no doubt is right,
> And more than right, but still, a little grief
> Will do for most of us, in my belief . . . '
> "Our Host joined in. 'This Monk, he talks too loud;
> All about "Fortune covered with a cloud" . . .
> Let's have no more of it. God bless you, master,
> It's an offence, you're boring us, that's why!
> Such talk as that's not worth a butterfly,
> Gives no enjoyment, doesn't help the game,
> In short Sir Monk - Sir Peter - what's-your-name,
> I heartily beg you'll talk of something else.
> But for the clink and tinkle of those bells
> That hand your bridle round on every side,
> By my salvation, by the Lord that died,
> I simply should have fallen down asleep
> Into the mud below, however deep.
> Your story then would have been told in vain,
> For, quoting the authorities again,
> "When lecturers find their audiences decrease,
> It does them little good to say their piece."
> Give us a word or two on hunting, say.'
> 'No,' said the Monk, 'I'm in no mood today
> For fun. Ask someone else. I've said enough.' " [84]

One cannot but agree: it is an offence for a preacher to bore the congregation. Yet for all his faults, the Monk did have this virtue: he knew when he had said enough!

THE WHOLE COUNSEL OF GOD

Twenty-twenty vision, we are told, is as good as an eye can be. You will help your hearers to achieve that in spiritual things if you follow Paul's twenty-twenty (Acts 20:20)

---

[84] The Canterbury Tales, by Geoffrey Chaucer; tr. by Nevill Coghill; Penguin Classics, 1977.

"I never held back from saying what would be for your good, and I kept on preaching my message to you, both publicly, and teaching you from house to house."

To that bold assertion, Paul then added the words,

"I kept nothing back from you; I never hesitated to declare the whole counsel of God" (vs. 27)

Could there be a more worthy aim for any preacher? If you hope to make the same boast, then here are three things to avoid -

1. THE "FINAL ANSWER" SYNDROME

You are standing in front of a group of new Christians. They were converted under your ministry a few weeks ago, but now you must leave them. This may well be your last opportunity to address them. What will you say? How can you ensure that they will continue to serve God with joy? What essential truth, what last word of advice, will you leave with them?

You decide to look for guidance in the various paper-backs that are currently popular. At once you are confused, for you discover that many writers of life-style books are addicted to presenting solutions that are claimed to be the final answer to the problem of how to be a true Christian.

These authors exhort their readers to espouse the "deeper" life, or the "higher" life; or perhaps to embrace the "crucified" life, the "death-to-self" life, the "broken" life, or the "surrendered" life; or it may be to understand "positional truth", or to seize the life of "praise", or to follow this "message" or that!

All these books exhibit a "final answer" syndrome. They seek to structure each Christian's life around one central idea. They assume that every dilemma can be resolved through the application of a single principle.

(a) Searching The Books

Nonetheless, since you must leave some final instruction with your flock, you pick up one of them. Ah! this book teaches that God has created us for his glory alone, hence you dare not do anything for your own pleasure. You finish the book feeling that God has been painted as an egocentric monster. Perhaps the author forgot that Jesus said, "I came that **you** might have abundant life."

You try again. You can hardly believe your eyes. The plan this author presents could appeal only to someone who secretly wishes he was made of stone and not flesh. It runs something like this: your life is utterly worthless, so you must be rid of it altogether. Woe to you if you take even a breath in your own strength. Absolutely nothing good is left in you. You must now consciously live every hour in divine strength alone. You dare do nothing, nor want anything, large or small, significant or insignificant, unless you first pray and get a heavenly clearance. Every action, every moment, must be placed under divine scrutiny and control.

You feel this might be a great life-style for a puppet, but not for your converts, whom you hope will learn how to "stay alert, keep a firm faith, never lose heart, and stand in strength" (1 Co 16:13).

Once more you reach up to the shelf. This writer declares that the secret of a life of victory is to see that you are already "complete in Christ", free, victorious, whole. Everything you want to be you already are! This looks more promising. At least the writer is not laying on his readers the unbearable yoke of being miserable when they are happy or dead when they are alive! But hold! Something seems to be missing? A dimension that fills the pages of the NT is lacking here. This book contains no warning against failure, no practical instruction, no recognition of the fact that to be complete in Christ is not the same as being complete in yourself, nor is completeness in the heavenlies equivalent to completeness on earth. You already know that your flock has a righteous standing in heaven, but you are concerned about their practical state on earth. So you must try again.

You take up another book. This one is different. It is the latest book on the market. It has sold half a million copies. Everyone is excited about it. Thirstily you pore over its pages. An hour later there is a stricken look in your eye. You exclaim, "My God! Surely you won't want me to live like this!" The book says: every Christian is a walking egomaniac; you must kill this hideous selfishness; so banish the word "I" from your vocabulary; do nothing to please yourself, demand nothing for yourself, give place to everybody, and so eradicate your "ego". This is difficult to do. Very few are successful. "But," says the author, "I have achieved it." What an egocentric that man is!

You look through several more books. They all proclaim, "Here is the way; you must walk only this path." They all differ. For the average office worker, or housewife, for the ordinary Christian, these brilliant schemes are impractical. They may have been successful for their authors. They may suit people whose temperaments are the same as the author's. They may even present ideas that are soundly scriptural. But as universal panaceas they fail, for it is absurd to suppose that every difficulty faced by Christians can be resolved by the application of a single rule.

Actually, no single concept can solve all the problems of all Christians, nor even all the problems of one Christian. Christian life is not so simple. The issues are complex, the needs are various, each person is different, each situation is unique, each temperament is special, and the solutions are diverse.

(b) Paul's Advice

So you are still searching for a concise parting message to give your young converts. Where can you go? One reference remains: the Bible. Pity you didn't look there first! For there you find a man who faced your exact problem. It was Paul, who had to instruct a group of converts he might never see again. In a few words he needed to convey to his friends the essence of the gospel he had preached to them. What did he say? We are told that he

> *"strengthened the souls of the disciples, exhorting them to continue in the faith, and saying that through many tribulations we must enter the kingdom of God" (Ac 14:22; cp. also 20:17-35).*

No simplistic answer there! Only steady perseverance in faith, resolute adherence to the truth, and brave endurance through every difficulty!

Paul was no "hobby-horse" preacher. He did not ride one idea to death. He approached Christian life from an amazing variety of different perspectives. He refused to be tied to one concept as though it alone was the magic wand that could remove every difficulty. He preached the "whole counsel of God".

Like the other NT preachers, but unlike many modern preachers, Paul understood that hobby horses may be fun to ride, but in the end they can't take you anywhere except up and down! [85]

1. THE ENTERTAINMEN TSYNDROME

In order to keep the crowd coming preachers sometimes yield to the temptation to stick to sermons that never deviate from the simple; they strive always to be pleasant, practical, amusing - which may easily decay into mere "ear-tickling" (2 Ti 4:2-4). Such preaching is no doubt necessary, at least from time to time, so long as it does not seriously compromise the teaching of sound doctrine and a demand for true discipleship. But beware of becoming a pleaser of people rather than a pleaser of God.

A way to guard against this "itching-ear" peril is to deliver from time to time what the gifted American preacher William H. Willimon calls a sermon with "some size". He quotes from a 17th century work, The Reformed Pastor, by the Puritan divine, Richard Baxter, who declared that

> "it is most desirable that the minister should be of parts above the people so far as to be able to teach them, and awe them."

Then Baxter advised pastors "to preach sermons so large as to stall the understandings of congregations", and he said,

> "See that you ... feed them not with all milk but sometimes with stronger meat; for it exceedingly puffs them up with pride when they hear nothing from ministers but what they know already or can say themselves ... Not that I would have you neglect the great fundamental verities, or wrong the weak and ignorant people while you are dealing with such as these; but only when the main part of your sermon is as plain as you can speak, let some one small part be such as shall puzzle these self-conceited men; or else have one sermon in four or five on purpose for them ... and

---

85   This "Final Answer" section has been adapted from the "Preface" to my book Christian Life.

let them see that it is not your obscure manner of handling but the matter itself that is too hard for them, and so may see that they are yet but children that have need of milk, and that you would be more upon such higher points if it were not that their incapacity doth take you off." [86]

(a) Frightened of Failure?

Notice how in his preaching Jesus exemplified the principle of going beyond the grasp of the people. Sometimes he accommodated his teaching to the capacity of his audience, but just as often he chose not to do so. He deliberately taught in parables that left most of his hearers (including his own disciples) bewildered (Lu 8:10, and several other places). On other occasions his hard sayings caused deep consternation (Jn 6:52, 60, 66; and think also about the startling toughness of passages like Mk 9:43-48). Many times his followers struggled in vain to grasp what he was talking about (Mk 8:16-21; 9:9-10, 30-32; Lu 9:45; 18:34). If we used the same measure of success for Jesus that we are inclined to impose upon each other we would call him an unsuccessful communicator!

Perhaps our problem is that we are so terrified of failure we eagerly grab at any technique that promises to shield us from its pain. No such concern troubled Christ. He knew what the Father had given him to say (Jn 8:28), and he said it fearlessly, trusting that the Father would do with his message whatever suited heaven's purpose.

(b) Ruled by Opinion?

Perhaps, too, we take too much notice of public opinion, whereas only God's opinion should count. In this respect, many preachers are less wise than was the pagan emperor -

> "He who ignores what his neighbour is saying and doing
> and thinking, and cares only that his own actions should
> be just and godly, is greatly the gainer in time and ease.

---

86 Baxter, of course, had in mind the exasperated words of the apostle in Hebrews 5:11-14, where (vs. 11) he uses a derisive colloquial Greek expression that means "numskulls", "blockheads", or something equally derogatory.

> "A good man does not spy around for the black spots in others, but presses unswervingly on towards his mark." [87]

Find your own proper mark from God, and then press only toward that goal, refusing to be turned aside either by the approval or opposition of those around you.

(c) Laborers in the Word

Of course, if preachers should sometimes speak what stands beyond the grasp of their congregations, then they themselves must first labour hard in scripture. No lazy preacher can hope to present a sermon with real "size", a message that will "stall the understanding" of a congregation. Unhappily, as Dr Willimon also says, all too often we hear only sermons that demand little of us, sermons that "reduce the gospel to bumper-sticker slogans, or to three points so easy to recall that they are not worth remembering." [88]

(d) Obscurity or Profundity?

If you do choose to follow Richard Baxter's advice, make sure to heed also his further counsel: do not confuse profundity of concept with mere obscurity of speech. Here is an example. In English, the phrase "I don't get it" can be applied either to a failure to understand an idea, or to a failure to receive something. In this anecdote it carries both meanings. A government employee asked his superior for a raise, and was told,

> "Because of the fluctuational predisposition of the productive capacity of your position, and its peculiar juxtaposition in relation to government standards, it would be fiscally injudicious for me to advocate an increment to your salary."

> "I don't get it," responded the staff person.

> "That's right," said the manager.

---

87 The words are those of the Roman emperor Marcus Aurelius (121-180), admonishing himself in his personal diary. The Meditations of Marcus Aurelius; tr. by Maxwell Staniforth; Penguin Books, 1986.

88 From "The Christian Ministry" journal, July-August 1991, pg. 39.

In that dialogue only the language was obscure, not the idea! You probably feel as I do, that you have listened to more than your quota of sermons riddled with the same fault. It is a vice you should avoid as strenuously as possible.

3. THE FOUNT OF WISDOM SYNDROME

Few preachers are competent to address anything other than the gospel; the rest of us should stay away from politics, and other issues, especially those that are more a matter of personal opinion than of revealed truth. We ought to stick to scripture. Once the pulpit abandons the Bible it ceases to possess any relevance, its voice no longer deserves to be heard.

King Henry IV of France went with his court to the church of St Gervais in Paris on Christmas day in 1609 to hear a celebrated preacher. Flattered by the honour of such distinguished visitors the preacher cast aside his notes, spent some time eulogizing the king, and then began to advise the monarch how better to govern the nation. Henry listened politely, and at the end made no comment except to express surprise that the preacher had occupied less than his allotted sixty minutes. But the next day, going back to the same church, Henry accosted the minister and said -

> "My father, everyone expected that at this time you should be in the Bastille; but the opinions of the world and those of myself do not always go together. I am much obliged to you for the zeal you have shown for my salvation. Continue, I beg of you, to request it of God for me, and contribute to it yourself by your good advice. In whatever place, and at whatever time you shall see fit to give it to me, you will always find me well inclined to follow it. I have only one request to make of you, that you do not let your zeal get the better of your discretion when you see fit to give me advice in public ... On my part, I will bring to (your preaching) all that docility of which I am capable, and if my weaknesses will permit me to go with you, it will be more my fault than yours if I do not become the better. I

beg you now to continue with God's work and leave my
name aside." [89]

So ought every preacher let politicians govern, while they keep their
pulpits dedicated to God's work. Does that mean we should never
address social issues? No, for like the prophets of old, godly zeal may
require us to raise a passionate voice against injustice, violence,
oppression, immorality, and the like. But such protests are far removed
from turning the pulpit into a lectern from which to advocate or condemn
the policies of some political party. Your church should be open to
people of every political hue; your pulpit should be coloured by none of
them.

---

89 International History Magazine, September 1973; pg.104.

CHAPTER TEN:

GARDENS FOR GOD

A garden is a lovesome thing, God wot!
  Rose plot,
  Fringed pool,
  Ferned grot -
    The veriest school
    Of peace; and yet the fool
Contends that God is not -
Not God! in gardens! when the eve is cool?
  Nay, but I have a sign:
'Tis very sure God walks in mine! [90]

We know that God loves a lovely garden. The Bible tells us so. And he delights to walk there in the cool of the evening and reveal himself to his people. We preachers are makers of gardens - not of flowers, but of words. And can there be a garden without arrangement, planning, care, weeding, watering, and all that goes into turning a wilderness into a place of surpassing beauty? Where better is the loveliness of Christ reflected, the Fairest of Ten thousand (Ca 5:10), than in a perfect garden? Only in one place: a well-formed sermon, in which he, the Living Word becomes incarnate again through the spoken word. Our goal should surely be to craft each sermon in such a way that Christ himself will be pleased to walk in them, and through them to reveal his own transcendent beauty.

How should you go about doing this? What method, or plan, should you use?

APPROACHING THE TASK

You may be interested to know how I go about the task of creating a sermon. Although each sermon takes its own shape in its own way, there are some general rules that I follow fairly consistently -

---

90   T. E. Brown (1837-97).

1. CHOOSE THE THEME

I usually begin by asking myself what do the people need; where do they require correcting, instructing, encouraging, assisting? This is done, of course, in conjunction with prayer, asking the Father the same questions, and trying to open my mind to an answer from heaven.

The "theme" that comes into my mind may finally resolve into a topic or a text, or a combination of both - that is, a topic built around a text.

2. DEVELOP THE THEME

Here I would recommend several steps -

(a) RESEARCH YOUR THEME

Read everything you can about it, first from the Bible, and then from commentaries, dictionaries, encyclopaedias, and the like. At the end of this process I would usually have amassed several pages of notes, jottings, ideas, references, and so on.

(b) PONDER YOUR OUTLINE

I often spend half of my preparation time, and sometimes more, thinking about how to arrange the material, what shape to give it in order to build an effective outline. During that time I might develop and scrap several skeletons before finding one that seems to be "just right".

An outline is an aid to memory; it helps the people to follow the message better; it prevents the preacher from rambling; it allows better time control (one can assess the length of a message from its outline).

How necessary is an outline? Ask a different question: what turns a pile of materials into a fine house? What changes a heap of ingredients into a delightful meal? What makes a collection of sounds a wonderful piece of music? The answer lies in one word: **arrangement!** In the same way, a sermon outline can bring a tangle of ideas into a harmonious, nourishing, and strengthening word from heaven.

(c) SEARCH FOR CREATIVITY

A lack of creative thinking is a common failing among preachers, and should be lamented. So many times one listens in vain for an inventive, refreshing, or stimulating way of handling a subject. Not that the problem is new. Rather, like some other faults I have mentioned, this problem too is ancient. Aristophanes long ago drew attention to it in his play The Frogs. He tells how Dionysus had resolved to go down into Hades to converse with the dead playwright Euripides, because there were no living dramatists worthy of the name. But first, Dionysus raised the matter with his slave Xanthius and with his host Heracles, whereupon Heracles remonstrated with him –

> Her. But have you not a shoal of little songsters,
> Tragedians by the myriad, who can chatter
> A furlong faster than Euripides?

> Dio. Those be mere vintage-leavings, jabberers, choirs
> Of swallow-broods, degraders of their art,
> Who get one chorus, and are seen no more,
> The Muses' love once gained. But oh!, my friend,
> Search where you will, you'll never find a true,
> Creative genius, uttering startling things.

> Her. Creative? How do you mean?

> Dio. I mean a man
> Who'll dare some novel, venturesome conceit. [91]

Are you a "true, creative genius, uttering startling things"? Do you have a daring, venturesome mind, a brave heart? Such thinking demands intense concentration, unwavering dedication, extended solitude - that is, a willingness to be alone for hours at a time. Don't just accept the first outline arrangement that springs into your mind (unless it is obviously the "right" one). Think! Think! **Think! THINK!** Ponder your outline until you know you have developed a way of presenting your message that will grip the attention of your hearers and draw from them the response you desire.

(d) PREPARE TO WORK HARD

Once again, a good arrangement (or sermon outline) requires hard, disciplined, inventive thinking. Some preachers are naturally more gifted at this than others, and each person possesses more facility at some times than others; but hard work improves anyone.

---

91   "Conceit" here means a clever device, or inventive arrangement. Rogers, op. cit., pg. 86, 87.

The renowned theologian and philosopher H. Richard Niebuhr did not hesitate (says one of his former students) to hand back to disappointed scholars their laboriously composed theses, inscribed with the command, "Scribere, et rescribere, et rescribere, et rescribere, et rescribere!" What is true of a doctoral thesis is even more true of a sermon outline. Write it, and write it again, and yet again, until it is as perfect as you can make it! Indeed, hard work can lift even a mediocre performer to a level of excellence. Georgio Vasari tells the life of the Florentine painter and sculptor Andrea del Verrocchio (1435-88) -

> "Andrea was at once a goldsmith, a master of perspective, a sculptor, a woodcarver, a painter, and a musician. It must be admitted that the style of his sculpture and painting tended to be hard and crude, [92] since it was a product of unremitting study rather than of any natural gift or facility. But because of his intense studies and diligence, even if he had completely lacked any natural facility Andrea would have excelled in those arts. To produce perfect work, painters and sculptors need both application and natural talent: unless both these are present, the artist rarely reaches the first rank. All the same, application is the more important of the two, and as Andrea possessed it in abundance, more than any other craftsman, he is counted among our finest and most outstanding artists." [93]

That is an example we should all follow. Your talents may be small; but if you apply yourself to the task of becoming an artist with words, you will undoubtedly be able to reach a high level of competence, if not excellence. Surely we owe the Lord that duty?

BUILD YOUR RESOURCES

At all times collect ideas, anecdotes, quotations, themes etc, and keep them on file for later use. Across more than 40 years of ministry I have filled several filing cabinet drawers with a vast array of stories, poetry, quotations, covering almost every imaginable theme. I never read

---

92   Only to a professional eye. To an amateur such as your author, his work looks quite beautiful enough!
93   Op. cit. Vol. Two, pg. 33.

anything without having at hand a pen and some paper. If a significant thought, a useful idea, an apt illustration, presents itself to me, I write it down at once, before it is forgotten or mislaid, and file it under an appropriate heading. [94]

However, do make sure that the illustrations you use say what you intend. Learn from the teacher who tried to give a group of children a lesson on temperance. She put one worm in a glass of water, and another in a glass of alcohol; the worm in the water kept on swimming, but the worm in the alcohol died. Then she asked, "What can we learn from this?" A boy answered, "If you've got worms, drink alcohol!"

A reading program in fiction, history, poetry, drama, theology, indeed, every area of human endeavour and every aspect of human experience, is essential. I have always worked hard, and I devote few hours to leisure; yet I still find time to read well over a hundred books each year (not including reading my Bible right through once a year). I spread those books across a wide range of interest and information, reading late at night, or at meal times, or while travelling - in fact, whenever I can find an hour or two, here and there. You may not be, and need not be, such an avid reader as I am; but you must devote at least some time to the task if you wish to keep your ministry fresh and alive across a lifetime.

Let no one say there are not enough hours in the day. If you want to find time, you will. Work to a disciplined schedule, watch less television, waste fewer hours in non-productive activities. The minutes are there if you search for them.

Surely every preacher should heed Paul's injunction -

> *"Study hard, so that God will fully approve of you, because he knows you are a worker who has no reason to feel any shame, one who correctly expounds the Word of truth" (2 Ti 2:15*

We live in a self-indulgent time; habits of arduous study, of toilsome labour, seem to have become unfashionable. Perhaps the decay (as the following anecdote suggests) began long ago. Rabbi Elijah (1720-1797) was known as the "Vilna Gaon" (the Genius of Vilna - the Polish town

---

94 I have my own filing system that works well enough for me; however, there are several commercial systems on the market, which you might find useful.

where he was born). He is to religious Jews what Albert Einstein is to other people, the standard of intellectual brilliance. Just as people in our society might remark of a child who has less than towering intelligence, "He's no Einstein," so religious Jews will say, "He's no Vilna Gaon!" The Gaon deserved his title. At six years of age he was studying the Bible and the Talmud on his own, because his teachers could not keep up with him; and at seven he delivered a masterly discourse on the Talmud in Vilna's main synagogue.

> "Afterward, the Chief Rabbi interviewed him, suspecting that the 7-year old had been primed like an actor for the lecture. He quickly concluded that the young boy understood all the intricacies of the talk he had delivered."

By the time he reached adolescence, the Gaon had mastered nearly all the main Jewish religious literature. From then until his death at seventy-seven he kept a regime of studying 18 hours a day. One of his disciples asked him why he studied so constantly even though he had long ago committed to memory almost every major Jewish text. He replied -

> "If the Vilna Gaon studies Torah eighteen hours a day, the other rabbis in Poland will study ten. If the other rabbis in Poland study ten hours a day, then in the more enlightened climate of Germany the rabbis will study six. If the rabbis in Germany study six, then the rabbis in England will study two. And if the rabbis in England study two hours a day, the Jews of England will at least keep the Sabbath.

> "But, if the Vilna Gaon studies only ten hours day, then the other rabbis in Poland will study only six, and the rabbis in Germany only two, and the rabbis in England only half an hour. And if the rabbis in England study Torah only half an hour a day, what will become of the Sabbath observance of English Jewry?" [95]

---

95 Jewish Literacy, by Rabbi Joseph Telushkin; William Morrow & Co Inc, NY991; pg. 218 -219

The Gaon was plainly not highly impressed by the study-habits of 18th-century English rabbis! How would he measure yours?

COMPONENTS OF AN OUTLINE

A good outline will have:

<u>colour</u>: interest, drama, impact, curiosity value

<u>unity</u>: each part belonging; nothing extraneous or irrelevant (it must be more than just three or four sermonettes strung together)

<u>sequence</u>: each section flowing naturally into the next (give attention to the "links" in your outline)

<u>balance</u>: no one part having disproportionate space (don't overemphasise unimportant points)

<u>conclusion</u>: the beginning and end should both be planned (the end, in fact, may be more important than the beginning; make it a true climax, not a feeble anti-climax.)

TYPES OF SERMONS

All preaching must, in one way or another, be an exposition of scripture, else it is not true preaching. Our duty is to expound scripture truthfully, apply it to the lives of the people, and draw them to full discipleship under the lordship of Christ. This book is not the place to enlarge upon the rules of hermeneutics, but let me at least say this:

- the expositor's first task is to discover the actual meaning of each passage, free of assumptions, prejudice, dogma, inference, and importations

- each passage must be allowed to speak for itself, so that while its meaning may be enriched or clarified by using other passages, it can never be altered (as is often done, for example, by those who set up various eschatological structures)

- remain faithful to the historical, biblical, and cultural context of the passage; that is, answer the question: "what meaning would have been conveyed to the first readers of this passage, given the identity of its author, the time it was written, its religious, social, and political background, the words that were used, and the subject it deals with?"

- how does the passage relate to Christ and the gospel?
- in what way should it be applied to modern hearers?

Having done your duty well as an expositor of scripture, then comes the task of choosing how to arrange your material. That will be the theme of the next chapter.

CHAPTER ELEVEN:

FLESH AND BONES

Lord Avonmore once said this about the celebrated 18th century English jurist, Sir William Blackstone -

> "He it was that first gave the law the air of a science. He found it a skeleton, and clothed it with life, colour, and complexion; he embraced the cold statue, and by his touch it grew into youth, health, and beauty." [96]

Without both flesh and bones, what is a man? Nothing but a rag doll, or a cold stone statue, or a museum piece. But put flesh and bones together, and you have a living person! That is what Sir William was said to have done with English law. He had a skeleton and added flesh. Your task is the reverse. You have a handful of "flesh" - all the material you have collected for your sermon - now you must add a skeleton, so that it can stand up on its feet! Put the two together well, and your sermon will have "life, colour, complexion, youth, health, and beauty"!

How should you do that? What kind of "skeleton" do you need?

Across the centuries sermon styles and structures have changed. Here are some that at various times have dominated pulpit practice -

RUNNING COMMENTARY

1. CHRYSOSTOM (circa 347-407)

> "Even when severely rebuking, when blazing with indignation, he never seems alien, never stands aloof, but throws himself in among them, in a very transport of desire to check, and rescue, and save. Is there, indeed, any preacher, ancient or modern, who in these respects equals John Chrysostom? . . . The early Christians disliked to hear, or make, a smoothly symmetrical and elegantly finished oration, like those of the secular

---

96   Cited from Familiar Quotations, by John Bartlett; 1980 edition; pg. 365.

orators. They wished for more familiar and free addresses, such as we call a prayer-meeting `talk'; and this was precisely the meaning of their words `homily' and `sermon'. The preacher took up his passage of scripture - usually somewhat extended - in a familiar way, sentence by sentence, with explanations and remarks, as he saw occasion; sometimes we find Chrysostom actually returning to go over the passage again, that it may suggest further remarks. At length, he would be apt to seize upon some topic of doctrine or practice which the text had directly or indirectly suggested, and discuss that by way of conclusion, not infrequently wandering off into the thoughts which one after another occurred." [97]

Another writer provides this description of Chrysostom, and it is one that all preachers might take as a standard -

"(Whatever defects he may have had were) overborne by his virtues: the fullness of scripture knowledge, the intense earnestness, the fruitfulness of illustration and application, the variation of topics, the command of language, the elegance and rhythmic flow of his Greek style, the dramatic vivacity, the quickness and ingenuity of his turns, and the magnetism of sympathy with his hearers. He knew how to draw in the easiest manner spiritual nourishment and lessons of practical wisdom from the Word of God, and to make it a divine voice of warning and comfort to every hearer. He was a faithful preacher of truth and righteousness and fearlessly told the whole duty of man. If he was too severe at times, he erred on virtue's side. He preached morals rather than dogmas, Christianity rather than theology, [98] active, practical Christianity that proves itself in holy living and dying. He was a martyr to the pulpit, for it was chiefly

---

97 Post-Nicene Fathers, vol 13; pg iv.
98 Not that his sermons are doctrinally light; on the contrary, he did not hesitate, when the occasion called for it, to elaborate the most profound aspects of Christian theology.

his faithful preaching that caused his exile (and subsequent death)." [99]

2. MARTIN LUTHER (1483-1546)

He was a great exponent of the "running commentary" style: "He never used much in the way of formal outline, but was strong on **explanation, argument, illustration, imagination, application**."

3. LANCELOT ANDREWES (1555-1626)

One of the last renowned practitioners of this style was bishop Lancelot Andrewes, who played an important part in the preparation of the King James Version of the Bible (published in 1611). Typical of the time, his preaching was full of learned quotations, scholarly allusions, clever puns, and the like. Yet only 100 years later, when preaching fashions had already changed, John Aubrey was able to say of him -

> "He had not that smooth way of oratory as now. It was a shrewd and severe animadversion [100] of a Scottish lord who, when King James asked him how he liked Bishop Andrewe's sermon, said that he was learned, but he did play with his text, as a jackanapes [101] does, who takes up a thing and tosses and plays with it, and then he takes up another, and plays a little with it - `here's a pretty thing, and there's a pretty thing!'" [102]

4. OUR OWN TIME

This style is becoming popular again, perhaps because it demands less mental effort from the people, whose attention span, under the impact of television, is growing increasingly shorter. The main thing is to avoid superficiality, that is, merely skimming over the surface of the passage, saying no more than is already obvious to any intelligent reader.

Notice again the five areas in which Luther (whose preaching was mainly a "running commentary" on scripture) was "strong": explanation,

99   The Post-Nicene Fathers, Vol. Nine, pg. 22.

100 Used here in the meaning of "criticism". It shows that already, in King James' time, a demand was arising for a more structured sermon.
101 Monkey.
102 "Brief Lives," in loc.

argument, illustration, imagination, application. there was nothing casual or superficial about his ministry. His preaching arose out of a profound knowledge of scripture, and widespread learning in many other fields.

STRUCTURED EXPOSITION

This style of preaching uses formal outlines, complete with title, introduction, headings, sub-headings, and conclusion. One of the first, and one of the greatest, to use this method was the great Puritan commentator Matthew Henry (1662-1714). For example, when I first prepared these notes, I opened Volume Three of his commentary at random, and fell at once upon the example given just below (# One).

Across the following decades, sermon outlines gradually became more formal, and more balanced in their shape (see example # Two below), until this structured style of preaching reached its fullest development in the latter part of the last century. Since then it has flourished for nearly a hundred years, but it may now be undergoing a decline. It has one major fault: a tendency to become too artificial and to lose dynamic.

Here are the two examples of a structured outline -

EXAMPLE ONE
From Matthew Henry's Commentary

PSALM 57:7-11

(i) **Introductory remarks.**

(ii) **How he prepares himself for the duty of praise** (vs 7)

      a. with reference to God's providence

      b. with reference to the worship of God

(iii) **How he excites himself to the duty of praise** (vs 8)

      - explanations and comment

(iv) **How he prides himself in the work of praise** (vs 9)

      a. his own heart was enlarged in praising God

      b. he desired to bring others to praise God

(v) **How he furnishes himself with matter for praise** (vs 10)

      - explanations and comment

(vi) **How he leaves it at last to God to glorify his own name**
      (vs 11)

Note how that outline is partly formal, partly formless; it represents a stage in the development of a carefully structured outline. However, if a structured outline is going to be used at all, the modern tendency would be to give it more colour and shape, thus . . .

EXAMPLE TWO

PSALM 57:7-11, 4

INTRODUCTION

- here is an amazing thing: a man untroubled, although he is surrounded by "lions"! (vs 4)

(A) MY HEART IS STEADFAST ON EARTH (vs 7)

- the key is praise, which must be:

    1. personal (vs 7)

    2. prevenient (vs 8)

    3. public (vs 9)

- such praise is possible only when we can affirm of God that:

(B) THY LOVE IS STEADFAST IN HEAVEN (vs 10)

- serenity comes from knowing that the love of God is

    1. powerful ("great to the heavens")

    2. providential (his "clouds" symbolise abundance)

    3. punctilious (he is "faithful")

CONCLUSION (vs 11)

- a confident prayer, affirming God's triumph in heaven and on earth.

NOTE: some would consider that outline too formal, or too artificial to represent David's passionate outpourings. Note also that it represents a thematic treatment of the passage (praise finding its source in love), rather than an exposition of what David actually said. Which leads on to our next type -

THEMATIC OR TOPICAL

The Bible is full of various themes, or topics, which can be plucked out of scripture and discussed on their own merits. For this task a "topical concordance" is a virtual necessity. One of the first to use this method systematically was Jean Claude, a 17th century Frenchman.

LIFE SITUATIONS

Situation sermons find their origin in some current incident (cp. Ac 2:16; 17:23). Or, they may draw upon a current problem or need, in either the church or society. But beware of becoming too personal, of embarrassing or offending someone!

If your sermon arises out of a situation in which a particular person is involved, then you need to be very sure either to keep the person's identity well hidden, or to ensure that he or she has no objection to the matter being aired in public.

BIOGRAPHICAL

Many great sermons have been built around one of the characters from the Bible, or around some Christian hero from church history.

THEOLOGICAL

Every pastor should take his or her people through the great doctrines of the Christian faith, spanning the entire range of basic truth, from the nature and being of God to the Second Advent of Christ and beyond.

You may use any or all of those sermon types; but always remain true to yourself, to your own personality and style. For example (if you will allow me to use myself again as an illustration), I seldom preach any kind of biographical sermon; somehow I just don't handle them well. Nor do I often expound extended passages of scripture. Most of my preaching, the kind I do best, is either based upon just a few words or lines of scripture, or upon a theme or topic.

OUTLINE METHODS

A sermon must attempt seven things:

- begin with a deeply felt truth

- justify it from scripture

- explain it in modern terms

- illuminate it with illustration

- make it memorable

- apply it to a current scene or need

- invite a suitable response.

There are various ways to achieve those goals -

Apply the text to: Self, Neighbour, and God

> e.g., The Fruit of the Spirit (Ga 5:22-23): the first three toward God; the second three toward your neighbour; the third three toward yourself.

Apply the text to: The World, the Church, the Individual

> e.g., The Return of Christ: how it will affect the world, the church, and you.

Ask the questions: who, what, why, when, where, how?

> e.g., "Arise and be baptised, washing away your sins!" - who should be baptised, by what command, etc?

Develop comparisons: from something to something

> e.g., "To turn them from darkness to light"- think of various ways to apply that statement, such as: from sickness (darkness) to health (light); from defeat to victory; from despair to hope; etc.

Arrange the text in a uniform pattern. For example, The Shepherd Psalm could be arranged thus -

Outline One: My Shepherd gives me Provision (1-2), Propitiation (3), Protection (4-5), and Promotion (6).

Outline Two: I shall not want: Pasture, Peace, Pathway, Protection, Preparation, Promise.

Outline Three: The Shepherd each day: feeds the sheep; guides the

sheep; comforts the sheep; brings the sheep safely home.

Outline Four: <u>A Table of</u>: Plenty in the Presence of Poverty (1-2); Salvation in the Presence of Sin (3); Life in the Presence of Death (4-5); Eternity in the Presence of Time (6).

Apply the text to various areas:

e.g., "From glory to glory": that is, from the glory of the law to the glory of the gospel; from the glory of the new birth to the glory of full stature; from the glory of a servant to the glory of a son; from the glory of the church to the glory of the kingdom.

e.g., "That in all things Christ might have preeminence": over the world, the church, the family, myself.

Develop the meaning of a word or idea:

e.g., He 7:25: the Greek word translated "uttermost" is applicable to time, position, or character; thus: An Undying Salvation (time); An Unchanging Salvation (position); A Universal Salvation (character).

e.g., "The Four Kinds Of Love": platonic, erotic, family, divine.

e.g., "The Four Kinds Of Faith": providential, saving, particular, gifted.

e.g., Mt 5:48: where the word "perfect" has the idea of "not yet complete, but advancing toward the goal;" thus: advancing toward maturity in God; advancing toward fellowship with God; advancing toward the purpose of God; and advancing toward surrender to God.

e.g., 1 Jn 1:3-4, "Fellowship" - what is this fellowship; what is its basis; what are its limits; what are its benefits?.

e.g., <u>check the dictionary definitions</u> of such words as peace, meekness, grace, blessing, virtue, holiness; etc; also use your thesaurus and theological dictionary.

Here are some more outlines, contrasting a more informal with a formal style -

Matthew Henry on Cl 3:1-6

<u>Introduction</u>: we must live such a life as Christ lived here on earth and lives now in heaven, according to our capacities -

    (A)   He explains this duty
    (B)   He assigns three reasons for this -

(1) that we are dead to present things
(2) our true life lies in the other world
(3) at the return of Christ we hope for happiness
   - Christ is a believer's life
   - Christ will appear again
   - we shall appear with him in glory
(C) He exhorts them to mortify sin
   (1) the lusts of the flesh
   (2) the love of the world
   (3) we kill them, or they kill us.

A MODERN OUTLINE ON THE SAME PASSAGE

Introduction: the sins listed in vs 5-8 are a terror to many Christians, but Paul has an answer to them -

(A) A Great Affirmation
   (1) Dead with Christ
   (2) Risen with Christ
   (3) Hidden with Christ

(B) A Great Application
   (1) The problem: is this true of me?
   (2) The solution: learn to say what God says!

(C) A Great Anticipation
   (1) What Christ is now, will show when he comes
   (2) What you are now will show when Christ comes
   (3) So begin now to affirm what you anticipate!

(D) A Great Admonition
   (1) Seek those things that are above
   (2) Set your affections on things above
   (3) Mortify your earthly members, which requires:
      - a decision to have complete victory
      - a confession that you have complete victory

Finally, note this pithy piece, told by Jack Hayford to a group of pastors (I was there) -

A hen was weary of laying her eggs in the same old place. She suggested various alternatives to the rooster, who rejected them all because they had been tried before. She finally suggested a nearby freeway. He commended her daring, but added this advice: "Lay it on the line, do it in a hurry, and get out of there!"

PRACTICUM

1. VOICE DEVELOPMENT

(a) It is possible to improve your voice in 4 areas:

Pitch. Use as low and melodious a level as you can reach without strain. Low-pitched tones are always more pleasant to listen to than high-pitched or harsh tones. Consciously pitch your voice low when you get up to speak. Many people out of nervousness, or because they wrongly think they will be heard more clearly, raise their normal voices two or three tones when they preach. This does great harm to the voice and is unpleasant to listen to. But don't make the mistake of straining the other way. You can do just as much harm to your vocal chords by trying to speak too low as by raising it too high. Whatever your normal conversational tone is will probably be about right.

Surprisingly, perhaps, you can develop low tones in your vocal range by speaking for a while in very high-pitched falsetto tones. Begin by speaking some sentence as low-pitched as you can. Then try the same sentences in falsetto. Then once again as low-pitched as you can. You will almost certainly find that your voice has lowered noticeably.

Compass: ranging from high tones to low. Whatever pitch you begin with will probably hold you firm for your entire sermon. It takes strong conscious effort to change the set pitch of your voice once you have begun to preach. If you start too high, you will find yourself squeaking when you try to speak up for emphasis; if you start too low you will have nowhere to go when you drop your voice. But if you learn your best range, so that you can begin a little below your middle level, then you will have plenty of room at both ends of the scale to create emphasis by raising and lowering your voice. In a well-delivered message you should range continually across your entire vocal compass.

Volume: controlled softness and loudness, which should come, not from your tonsils, but from your diaphragm (see below).

Penetration: this is not the same as volume, but comes rather from the way you project your voice. With good penetration a whisper will be heard as easily as a shout. This comes from using your diaphragm, from speaking from the forward part of your mouth, from looking your audience in the eye, and from directing your attention to the back row of your audience (at least when you first start speaking).

(b) Control the flow of air.

Not by your lungs, but by using your diaphragm. This is the muscle that should ache, not your throat, after a vigorous sermon. All force should come from the diaphragm, which you naturally use when coughing, laughing, yawning, or breathing while lying on your back. It is the great muscle that sits like an inverted dinner plate between your chest cavity and your abdomen. If you are unsure what and where it is, lie on your back, put your hand on your stomach, and breathe heavily. You will feel the muscle expand and contract. All breathing (whether you are prone or upright) should come from movement of the diaphragm, not from chest movement. If you breathe from your chest you will never get enough air into your lungs. Your shoulders should not rise and fall when you breathe; instead, if you are breathing properly, your stomach will move in and out!

Loudly and vigorously speak the syllable: Chow! letting all the force come from your diaphragm. Learn the "feel" of that action, keep practising until you use it continually, without thinking.

(c) Resonate your voice

Resonate your voice from the hard palate at the top of your mouth, not from the fleshy back parts of the throat (which is a sure way to tear your throat to pieces). Some sounds come naturally from the hard palate and resonate in the upper bony structure: Oo! Let! Contrast those sounds with a throaty Ah! Then, without changing the position of the sounds, say in succession, Oo! Ah! Oo! Ah! You will notice that the "ah!" is now coming from the front part of your mouth, not from the back. I often lecture vigorously for six or seven hours in a row, but seldom have any problems with my voice, because I have practised, and keep on using, these techniques.

(d) To develop resonance

To develop resonance, begin by humming, then pronounce the syllable Maw! Feel the roof of your mouth, and your entire cranium, vibrating.

(e) Develop variety

Develop variety by the following formula:

- higher - lower
- softer - louder
- faster - slower.

In the earlier years of our marriage I nearly drove my wife crazy by prowling around the house with Dante's Inferno in my hands, reading it aloud and following the above formula. That is, I would read a line or two as high-pitched as I could, then the next couple of lines very low, then soft, then loud, then quickly, then slowly, and on and on, constantly mixing those six items together in various combinations. I did the same with the Book of Psalms.

2. OUTLINE PRACTICE

(1) Develop a sermon outline on one of the Psalms. Your outline will be discussed in class, and then various other ways of outlining the Psalm will be suggested.

(2) Prepare a 3-minute "talk to get action". Your talk must have 3 parts:

(a) a moving or dramatic incident from your own life (2 minutes)

(b) something you want the people to do (30 seconds)

(c) the benefit they can expect (30 seconds)

- e.g., "A powerful day of prayer and fasting I once enjoyed .... You too should have such a day .... These are the benefits you will gain .... "

(3) Find in a book, commentary, or reference Bible, an outline of the Twenty-Third Psalm, and copy it out, with the source.

(4) Develop an outline of your own on a selected passage of scripture.

(5) Prepare a 5-minute talk, which must contain

- Introduction
- Two or three major headings
- Two or three subheadings under each major heading
- Application and Conclusion

    (a) A strict time-limit will be enforced

    (b) You may read the talk, use notes, or speak extemporaneously; but in any case, be animated, look at your audience, speak from your heart.

CHAPTER TWELVE:

CHRIST INCARNATE

"Bind my words upon your heart for ever, and fasten them firmly around your neck" (Pr 3:3; 6:21).

When Moses gave Israel the laws of God he told the people to make bracelets for their wrists, and forehead bands, into which passages of scripture had been worked (De 6:8-9). He also told them to carve the words of the Law onto the doorways of their homes, and upon their gateposts. These public displays were a demonstration of their absolute commitment to the Word of God. Nothing must ever be allowed to separate them from that Word. Going out and coming in, awake or asleep, at work or play, whether resting at home or travelling abroad - always they were to be clothed with scripture, bearing it upon their persons, and marking it upon their homes. In a sense, they were to live, move, and sustain their very life within the ever-present parameters of the divine oracles.

Devout Jews, as nearly as they can in the modern world, still obey those rules. If you stand at the front door of many Jewish homes, you will discover a little niche, perhaps set in the wall, with a tiny door, and behind the door a small scroll upon which some portion of the Law is printed. But what does this have to do with our text?

If you read the context in Proverbs you will realize that Solomon, some five hundred years after Moses, echoed the great Lawgiver's words, except that he gave them a surprising twist. Where Moses talked about "wrists", and "foreheads", the king preferred "hearts" and "necks". Now it is a brave Jew who dares to re-write Moses! How did Solomon find such boldness? Why did he so brazenly change the ancient text?

Probably, because he had observed a fault that is equally common in our own day: people attach themselves to the Bible readily enough, yet never allow it to get past their skin. They wear it only on the surface of their lives. They never truly bend their neck beneath it, nor cherish it deep in their hearts, nor avidly devour it with their eyes. Solomon was appalled when he saw people wearing scripture merely as a piece of religious decoration, or using it only as a pleasant tradition. He wanted to shock his readers out of apathy and ritual, and bring them into a different kind of life-transforming relationship with scripture. Which means -

A FERVENT LOVE OF SCRIPTURE

"Bind my words around your heart for ever."

What do you really feel about your Bible? Many people are fond of their Bibles for no better reason than they will never buy a more expensive book. They also like the tactile pleasure the book gives them, when they feel its fine leather cover, and admire its gilt-edged pages. Perhaps too, family tradition requires them to have at least one Bible in the house; indeed, they could hardly bear not to have a Bible sitting on the shelf, or beside their bed, or on a coffee table. They gain from it a sense of comfort, or security, a kind of Christian version of a good luck charm. Others like to carry their Bible to church on Sunday, and are pleased when they know where to find the text for the day's sermon. They revere its antiquity, and its central place in our civilization; they would be disappointed if no portion of it were read aloud in church, or at a funeral or wedding. But do they ever read the book themselves? Is scripture in the end little more to them than a pious adornment, akin to the bracelets and frontlets the ancient Jews wore, or to the jewelled crosses some Christians wear?

Someone might protest (I have even had pastors say this to me): "But why should I love the Bible; why do I have to read it all the time?" There are three fine reasons why your Bible should be your greatest earthly treasure, why it should occupy a supreme place in your estimation and joy, and why you should "bind it around your heart for ever!" -

THE FACE OF GOD IS MIRRORED IN SCRIPTURE

Nowhere but in the God-breathed pages of scripture (2 Ti 3:16) can you find a true image of God. All other divine likenesses are either human or demonic fabrications, and may lead to idolatry. Anyone who conceives an image of God outside of scripture must inescapably make a deity in their own likeness, who will bear scant resemblance to the real God.

Whatever concept of God each Christian has must be thoroughly shaped and controlled by scripture.

Did you have a vision of God? Did you see him in a dream? Did you have some other numinous encounter with the divine? If what you saw, or felt, conforms to scripture, then you may welcome and rejoice in it. But no dream or vision, nor any apparition, nor a seeming manifestation from heaven, nor a supernatural oracle, deserves your acceptance if it conjures up a picture of God that departs from the Bible. God is most present to a believing heart when his glory springs out from the inspired page.

Do you want to meet with God? Turn to your Bible. Do you want to be shaped into his likeness? Turn to your Bible. Do you want to encounter his splendour and holiness? Turn to your Bible! All that can be seen and known about God in this world is comprehended in scripture! He is truly alive in scripture, waiting to reveal himself to those with eyes to see, and ears to hear, and a heart to believe!

Especially, of course, the face of God is mirrored in the person and life of Jesus, and therefore above all in the gospel. No clearer vision is possible. No other vision is comparable. Those who gaze upon Christ through the gospel will change Philip's request into an affirmation: "I have been shown the Father, and I am satisfied!" (Jn 14:8-9).

THE COMMAND OF GOD IS SPOKEN IN SCRIPTURE

Here is the voice, and finally the only voice, of authority. No command is binding upon me unless it speaks in conformity with scripture, nor can any truth surpass what is revealed here. I can allow no other rule establish the framework of my life. What scripture commands, I obey. What scripture forbids, I shun. What scripture teaches, I believe.

If you would know the will of the Father, then where else should you turn except to his own Word? Why would you seek any other authority, or look for any other endorsement? If God has spoken plainly in scripture, why would you want another opinion, or hope for a better way? If the Bible says it, that settles it!

Now I know how hard it can be sometimes to discover just what the Bible does say, and how many conflicting voices keep on demanding attention. [103] So many different opinions! So many contrary doctrines! But the more earnestly you search the scriptures, the more easily you will learn to recognize the Father's true voice (Jn 5:39; 10 :4). At any rate, this much is sure: any voice that speaks against scripture can be and should be ignored.

THE PROMISE OF GOD IS REVEALED IN SCRIPTURE

How will you ever know what sweet blessings, what gracious gifts, what inexpressible joys the Father wants to pour into your life unless you search the Bible? (Jn 5:39; Ac 17:11) All other sounds are uncertain, but this one is sure -

> *"Not one word has ever failed of all the good promise that he has spoken" (1 Kg 8:56); and again, "God is not a man who might lie, nor a mortal who might change his mind; what he has promised he will do, and what he has spoken he will perform!" (Nu 23:19).*

But no promise spoken outside of scripture has any infallible validity. All other prophecies, oracles, dreams, visions, voices, must be tested before you dare give them your trust (1 Co 14:29; 1 Th 5:20-21; 1 Jn 4:1). Even then, you should handle them with caution, unless they clearly echo some part of scripture. Only the Bible speaks with a voice that can be unequivocally trusted by anyone, anywhere, in any situation.

But how can a person who leaves the Book closed ever discover any of those good things? If you wish to see the face of God mirrored, and hear the command of God spoken, and find the promise of God revealed, then you yourself must read the sacred page. "But," says someone, "surely it is enough to go to church and hear sermons?" No, for you could go to church every day for the rest of your life, yet still hear only a small part of scripture. I have been preaching now for 60 years. Suppose I had depended only on my sermons to show me the face of God, and to reveal to me his command and his promise? Much of what the Lord has wanted to say to me personally would have remained unheard and unknown. If you want to grasp every part of God's will for your life, if you want to

---

103 My book on hermeneutics, "Understanding the Bible," addresses this question.

benefit from every promise that belongs to you in Christ, then you yourself must read through and through the Bible. There is no other way to gain those benefits. Multitudes of Christians are broken and beaten, confused and distraught, simply because they keep their Bibles shut. Therefore they never hear more than a part of what God wants to command them, nor receive more than a part of what he wants to give them.

Such people should heed the counsel of Solomon: "Bind my words around your heart for ever!" - that is, let the Bible become your chief treasure on earth, and its words your fondest desire (Jb 23:12; Ps 19:10; 119:103,127; Je 15:16).

A DISCIPLINED STUDY OF SCRIPTURE

"Fasten my words around your neck."

Those words could have produced only one image in the ancient world: a picture of a slave market, and of a newly purchased slave being dragged over to the waiting blacksmith to have an iron collar welded around his or her neck. Once it was in place, the collar could not be removed. The slave had to bear its chafing weight year after year, a life-long necklace of indenture, a sign of perpetual bondage.

From that striking metaphor we can learn three things about our relationship with scripture. We must submit ourselves to the -

DEDICATED SERVICE OF SCRIPTURE

Listening to some Christians, one could be forgiven for thinking that the Bible should serve our will, instead of the reverse. Solomon had no doubt about the true condition. As surely as slaves must bend their wills to that of their owner, so we must place our necks in the collar of scripture. Do you heed the Bible only when it is easy to do so, or comfortable, or pleasant? Do you abandon the Bible whenever it seems to speak harshly, or to demand too much, or to deny some fancy of your own? Then you are no servant of the Word of God, nor can you claim to be obedient to the command to "fasten it around your neck".

There are those who insist that "they believe the Bible from cover to cover". But how much is that worth, if they refuse to obey it?

Then there are others who tell me they would read the Bible gladly, if only it were enjoyable. "But," they say, "so much of it is dull, and hard to understand. I find it so boring and confusing. I once decided to read a chapter a day, but I just couldn't keep it up!" Here is a remarkable thing! A slave choosing to engage only in what is amusing! What folly! Even if the entire Bible tasted like sand in your mouth, or were less digestible than a dinner of ashes, still you would be obliged to search its pages (2 Ti 2:15). Of course, no one can truly say that the Bible is a barren desert. Many parts of scripture are joyously delightful to read, filled with ecstasy for the soul, rapture for the spirit, and instruction for the mind. Yet not all. For other places can be weariness to the soul, and tedium to the mind; and sometimes a passage that once seemed wonderful can today seem utterly bleak. Nonetheless, we cannot choose to read only what is easy, for -

> "*All* scripture is in-breathed by God, and is beneficial
> for instruction, for rebuke, for guidance, and for gaining
> mastery in righteousness" (2 Ti 3:16).

Discipline is required here, to grapple resolutely with "all" scripture, omitting nothing of the divine counsels. Sometimes that discipline may seem harsh, and the words of scripture unpalatable, so that your soul groans beneath the burden. Should you then make a bid for freedom and try to loose your neck from scripture's collar? Hardly! Those who cast off the seeming yoke of the Word of God will soon find themselves enmeshed in real bondage, while those who bind themselves to serve scripture will find perfect liberty! Long after Solomon's time another teacher in Israel took up the metaphor of enslavement to the Word of God, and saw in that apparent bondage the only real freedom -

> "Lock your feet into wisdom's fetters, and fasten her
> collar around your neck. Bend your shoulder under her
> burden, and do not complain about her chains. Yield
> yourself to her with all your heart, and bring all your
> strength into her service. ... The day will come when
> instead of toil she will give you rest, and in place of
> sorrow joy. You will find that her manacles have been
> turned into a strong wall around you, and her collar has
> changed into a beautiful garment. Like a royal sash over
> an imperial robe, so will her chains become. Her yoke
> will adorn you like a precious ornament. She will place
> herself upon your head like a golden crown.

"If you are willing, my son, you can learn discipline, and if
you work hard you will become wise. If you love to listen
you will amass knowledge; if you submit to teaching, you
will increase in skill." [104]

You know the saying, "there is no gain without pain." It applies to the
study of the Bible. Those who want gold, must dig for it. Sapphires and
rubies do not lie scattered upon the ground. "By the sweat of your
brow," says God, "you will eat bread" (Ge 3:19), and the earth yields her
riches only to those who toil for them. But God is willing for earth's
hidden hoard to be found, especially by his "anointed" who dig deeply
into the pliant soil of scripture -

> "I will give you the riches that are buried in darkness,
> and you will find the wealth that is hidden in secret
> places" (Is 45:3). [105]

Have you fastened the Word of God like a slave's collar around your
neck? Then you will accept the task of digging for its riches, and you
will submit wholly to its dictates. And whether it brings you pleasure or
pain, dullness or delight, you will embrace the discipline of reading your
Bible repeatedly from cover to cover; you will embark upon the duty of
constantly mining the sacred page for its divine ore. Which will mean
adopting a program of Devoted Reading of Scripture

You should read your Bible regularly, right through from beginning to
end, over and over again. Why should any Christian find that a tedious
duty? Should it not rather be one that we embrace gladly? Those who
love Christ, the Living Word, must surely love also the Bible, the
Written Word? Yet there is at least one reason why many people cannot
find any joy in scripture: it is called legalism. Every Bible reader must
guard against their reading become a "good work" by which they hope to
establish credit in heaven. You cannot accumulate some quotient of
righteousness by adding chapter upon chapter to your devotional

---

104 Sir 6:24-33. Sirach was a Jewish rabbi who wrote his Book of Wisdom
near the end of his life, circa 180 B.C. It was translated into Greek by his
grandson, circa 132 B.C.
105 He means, of course, Cyrus, to whom God was promising ownership of the
precious metals that are buried in the "dark" and "secret" places of the
earth. But we may apply it easily enough to a believer digging into the
Word of God.

program. No "good work" of ours - not prayer, fasting, giving, witnessing, church-going, Bible reading, nor anything else - can add so much as one hair to the righteousness that is already fully ours as God's gift in Christ (Ro 5:17; Ga 2:15-16). If we have any access to the throne, it is only by grace, through the precious blood (He 10:19-23). We have no merit to offer God save the goodness of Christ. We have only one plea: "I dare not trust the sweetest frame, but wholly lean on Jesus' name!"

> Why then read the Bible? Is there no advantage if I do
> read, and no loss if I don't?

Let another question provide the answer: do you receive benefit from the discipline of eating each day? Would you suffer loss if you stopped eating? Why do you eat? Certainly not to create righteousness, but to sustain good health. You are made neither more nor less righteous by eating or by abstaining from food. Again, did you have breakfast this morning? Will that bowl of cereal enhance your holiness? Or did you miss breakfast? Will your fast rob you of sanctity? Of course not! Neither does reading or not reading the Bible on a given day affect your status in heaven. But if you abstain from food for too long, your health will suffer, and you may even die. Likewise, starve your spirit of the Bread of Life, and it will inevitably sicken and grow weak.

Further, while you probably enjoy most of your meals, if for some reason eating became unpleasant, would you then stop eating? No, you would still feel obliged to force some nourishment into yourself. You eat, not only because you want to, but because you must! You probably also try to maintain a balanced diet, even if you find some necessary foods distasteful. So too with the Bible. Those who reject all except its sugary sweetmeats will suffer spiritual tooth decay. Gumless, as it were, they will be confined to the milk of the Word, and find themselves disgracefully unable to chew its meat (1 Co 3:2; He 5:11-14).

So then, you should commit yourself to a program of regular Bible reading, while remembering not to make a "law" out of it. Do not bind yourself to a suffocating routine, which you then become afraid to break in case you might offend God, or lose holiness. Happily, you will not lose much if you miss a day or two (or even more) here and there, nor will you gain much if you adhere scrupulously to a rigid calendar of readings.

Let me say it again: there is one sure way to make the entire Bible as dull as death. How? Just turn it into a legal regime by which you expect to gain better access to the throne of God. Instead of a righteous collar, scripture will then become a self-righteous millstone that will drag you down into the Pit.

God has declared emphatically that no one will ever be made righteous by the works of the law - not even by avid Bible reading! So keep your liberty in Christ; yet also keep reading your Bible, for in those sacred pages you will best discover the glory of Christ. Read as much as you can, as often as you can, until you get to the end, and then start again!

DISCIPLINED HEARING OF SCRIPTURE

Now we come to the most important part of this chapter, and possibly of this entire book.

Without diminishing in any way the importance of what I have written above, let me now say that nothing transcends in significance the need for Christians to gather with the church of God, and to hear the Bible preached. Why? Because

Christ, the Living Word, is incarnate in the Spoken Word.

There is a way in which Christ reveals himself through preaching that is not duplicated in any other aspect of Christian life. As Paul said, how can people call on someone in whom they do not believe, and how can they believe unless they hear, and how are they to hear until Christ is **preached**? (Ro 10:15). That is, there is a hearing about Christ, a quality of faith in him, and an experience of him, that arises primarily, and perhaps only, out of the pulpit.

Would you meet Christ face to face? Then go to church and hear the Word of God preached by someone who is full of grace, and who proclaims the truth in the power of the Holy Spirit! You will never have a finer revelation of Christ; you will never experience a closer encounter with him. Indeed, any supposed vision of Christ, any presumed experience of him, which does not have its root and origin in scripture, must be held suspect. Delusion comes swiftly when sound doctrine is discarded.

Why do you go to church? To hear a fine sermon? That is the tragedy of much modern church life. People have become sermon-tasters rather than Christ-meeters. They want their preachers to be amusing, lively, comforting, easy-on-the-ear, not confrontational nor demanding, not given to rebuke, nor offering difficult instruction. Congregations today resent expending any effort to listen to a sermon; rather, they expect to be borne along with it, on a tide of excitement. They hunt around for an entertaining orator rather than a plain teacher of plain truth. But notice here three things -

First: the command scripture lays upon preachers to teach the whole counsel of God, without fearing the face of man, nor favouring any, is compulsory (Ac 6:4; 1 Ti 4:6-16; 2 Ti 2:15; 4:2; Ti 1:13; 2:15; etc). But can any preacher meet that demand? If the people are unwilling to listen, how can the preacher speak? Fulfilment of the command to teach "sound doctrine" depends upon a congregation that is willing to sit patiently, earnestly, comprehendingly, at the preacher's feet. No congregation can offer any higher act of worship to God. Yet there are those who stand for an hour singing lots of merry or soulful songs, calling it deep worship, while they have no heart to hear and heed the teaching of sound doctrine. That is nothing but a pious pretence. We might even say that if there is an hour of "worship" there should be at least an hour of preaching! The pulpit, not the music rostrum, must stand highest in the church. Let nothing even seem to lessen its status; let nothing presume to claim higher honour. Jesus said, "Go into all the world and **preach**" - not sing, pray, worship, dance, or anything else. We should surely do all those things, do them abundantly, and do them well - but never at the cost of supplanting or even diminishing the pulpit.

Second: the incarnation of Christ in a sermon has nothing to do with cleverness. God has called very few true orators into the pulpit, because lofty rhetoric, spellbinding pulpiteering, has little to do with the purpose of preaching, which is to **reveal Christ**. Finely honed skills are not inimical to good preaching, and God does call some who are marvellously gifted. But they are few, and in the end such skills are unnecessary. The work can be admirably done by people with quite humble gifts, if they are rich in the grace of Christ, full of the Holy Spirit, and proclaim the Word of God plainly and trustfully. No Christian preacher could wish anything higher than that Christ himself should be brought to the people through a sermon. And if Christ is pleased to become incarnate through the spoken Word, how can the style of the sermon matter? But if Christ is absent from it, where is there any value in the most splendid oratory?

Third: congregations must be awakened again to the principle that Christ is incarnate in the spoken Word. They must be taught how to listen to a sermon: not for amusement, nor even instruction, but above all, to see Christ. If the people came to church expecting Christ to be present in the sermon, how eager they would be for the preaching to begin! Even more eager than the preacher is to start! How the pulpit would be honoured if the people knew that while they listened they would meet Christ face to face! How little they would care if their preacher was not a famous public speaker! How much they would uphold the sermon in prayer, so that they might see, and hear, and feel, more of Christ reaching out to them across the pulpit!

Perhaps you are yourself only mediocre in platform ability? What does it matter, and what more could the people want, if Christ is incarnate in your preaching? That should be the aspiration of every local church. That should be the hope of the pastor, and of every member of the congregation. Certainly preachers should study hard, and labour hard in every way to become good workers, approved by God, with no reason to feel ashamed about their work (2 Ti 2:15). But whether or not we can ever rise above the ordinary as speakers, let us strive in this to be utterly extraordinary: that Christ is alive in every word we speak, showing his grace and glory to the people of God.

METHODS OF BIBLE STUDY

BY R. A. TORREY

Adapted for the Online Bible by Larry Pierce [106]

The following selections are for your further instruction and guidance and are not intended for the purpose of examination but to assist you in the development of your sermon outlines and preparations.

REGULAR STUDY

Make up your mind that you will put some time EVERY DAY in the study of the Word of God. That is an easy resolution to make, and not a very difficult one to keep; if the one who makes it is in earnest. It is one of the most fruitful resolutions that any Christian ever made. The forming of that resolution and the holding faithfully to it, has been the turning point in many a life. Many a life that has been barren and unsatisfactory has become rich and useful through the introduction into it of regular, persevering, daily study of the Bible.

This study may not be very interesting at first, the results may not be very encouraging; but, if one will keep plugging away, it will soon begin to count as nothing else has ever counted in the development of character, and in the enrichment of the whole life. Nothing short of absolute physical inability should be allowed to interfere with this daily study.

It is impossible to make a rule that will apply to every one as to the amount of time that shall be given each day to the study of the Word. I know many busy people, including not a few labouring men and women, who give an hour a day to Bible study, but if one cannot give more than fifteen minutes a great deal can be accomplished. Wherever it is possible the time set apart for the work should be in the daylight hours. The very best time is in the early morning hours. If possible lock yourself in with God alone.

---

106 This study has been further modified by Ken Chant for use in Vision Christian College campuses, but remains basically the same as the original

DILIGENT STUDY

Make up your mind to STUDY the Bible. It is astounding how much heedless reading of the Bible is done. Men seem to think that there is some magic power in the book, and that, if they will but open its pages and skim over its words, they will get good out of it. The Bible is good only because of the truth that is in it, arid to see this truth demands close attention.

A verse must oftentimes be read and re-read and read again before the wondrous message of love and power that God has put into it begins to appear. Words must be turned over and over in the mind before their full force and beauty takes possession of us. One must look a long time at the great masterpieces of art to appreciate their beauty and understand their meaning, and so one must look a long time at the great verses of the Bible to appreciate their beauty and understand their meaning.

When you read a verse in the Bible ask yourself, *"What does this verse mean?"* Then ask:

> *"What does it mean for me?"* When that is answered ask yourself again: *"Is that all it means?"* and don't leave it until you are quite sure that is all it means for the present. You may come back at some future time and find it means yet a great deal more. If there are any important words in the verse weigh them, look up other passages where they are used, and try to get their full significance.

God pronounces that man blessed who *"meditates"* on the Word of God *"day and night."* (Ps 1:2,3). An indolent skimming over a few verses or many chapters in the Bible is not meditation, and there is not much blessing in it. Jeremiah said: *"Thy words were found and I did eat them."* (Je 15:16) Nothing is more important in eating than chewing. If one doesn't properly chew his food, he is quite as likely to get dyspepsia as nourishment. Don't let any one chew your spiritual food for you. Insist on doing it for yourself. Any one can be a student who makes up his mind to. It is hard at first but it soon becomes easy. I have seen very dull minds become keen by holding them right down to the grindstone.

As you meditate on each passage of Scripture, ask yourself, *"Is there*

- a sin I should keep a way from?"

- a promise I can call my own?"

- a command for me to obey?"

- a blessing I can enjoy?"

- a failure from which I can learn?"

- a victory for me to win?"

- a new " thought about God, the Lord Jesus, the Holy Spirit, Satan, man?"

- a truth in this passage that has greatly affected me?"

TOPICAL STUDY

STUDY THE BIBLE TOPICALLY. Take up the various subjects treated in the Bible, one by one, and go through the Bible and find what it has to say on these subjects. It may be important to know what the great men have to say on important subjects; it is far more important to know what God has to say - and usually a very small part - and so their ideas are very imperfect and one-sided. If they only knew all God had to say on the subject, it would be far better for them and for their friends.

The only way to know all God has to say on any subject is to go through the Bible on that subject. To do this it is not necessary to read every verse in the Bible from Genesis to Revelation. It would be slow work, if we had to do that on every subject we took up. This would be necessary were it not for *Text Books* and *Concordances.* But in these we have the results of the hard work of many minds. Here we have the various passages that bear on any subject brought together and classified for use, so that now we can do in a few hours what would otherwise take months or years.

The topical method of Bible study is simplest, most fascinating and yields the largest immediate results. It is not the only method of Bible study, and the one who pursues it exclusively will miss much of the blessing God has for him in the Bible. But it is a very interesting and fruitful method of study. It was Mr. Moody's favourite method. It fills one's mind very full on any subject studied. Mr. Moody once gave several days to the study of *"Grace."* When he had finished he was so full of the subject that he rushed out on the street and going up to the first man he met he said: *"Do you know anything about Grace?"* *"Grace who,"* the man asked. *"The Grace of God that bringeth salvation."* And then Mr. Moody poured out upon that man the rich treasures he had dug out of the Word of God.

That is the way to master any subject and get full of it. Go through the Bible and see what it has to say on this subject. You will soon have a long list of the various passages of Scripture that bear on your subject. Look them up one after another and study them carefully and see just what they are teaching you. When you have gone through them you will know far more about that subject than you ever knew before, and far more than you could learn by reading any books that men have written about it, profitable as many of these books are.

Sometimes it will be necessary to look up other subjects that are closely related to the one in hand. For example, you wish to study what the teaching of God's Word is regarding the atonement. In this case you will not only look under the head *"Atonement, "* but also under the headings of *"Blood", "Death of Christ. "* To do this work a concordance is not necessary but it is often very helpful.

There are four important suggestions to make regarding Topical Study of the Bible.

(1) ***BE SYSTEMATIC***. Do not take up subjects for study at random. Have a carefully prepared list of the subjects you wish to know about, and need to know about, and take them up one by one, in order.

If you do not do this, the probability is that you will have a few pet topics and will be studying these over and over until you get to be a crank about them, and possibly a nuisance. You will know much about these subjects, but about many other subjects equally important you will know nothing. You will be a one-sided Christian.

(2) ***BE THOROUGH***. When you take up a subject do not be content to study a few passages on this subject, but find just as far as possible every passage in the Bible on this subject.

(3) ***BE EXACT*** Find the exact meaning of every passage that deals with your chosen subject. The way to do this is simple:

(3.1) Note the exact words used.

(3.2) Get the exact meaning of the words used. This is done by finding how the word is used in the Bible. The Bible usage of a word is not always the common use of today. For example, the Bible use of the words "sanctification" and 'justification" is not the same as the common use.

(3.3) Notice what goes before and what comes after the verse. This will often settle the meaning of a verse when it appears doubtful.

(3.4) See if there are any parallel passages. The meaning of many of the most difficult passages in the Bible is made perfectly plain by some other passages that clarify them. The parallel passages are usually given in the margin of a good reference Bible and still more fully in a topical concordance.

(4) **_BE ORDERLY_**. That is, arrange the results of your topical study in an orderly way and write them down. One should constantly use pen and paper in Bible study. When one has gone through all the references on any subject, he will have a large amount of material, but he will want to get it into usable shape. For example, here is how a group of references on _Prayer"_ might be classified -

(a)   Who Can Pray

_____

_____

_____

(b)   To Whom to Pray

_____

_____

_____

(c)   For Whom to Pray

_____

_____

_____

(d) When to Pray

_____

_____

_____

(e) Where to Pray

_____

_____

_____

(f) For What to Pray

_____

_____

_____

(g) How to Pray

_____

_____

_____

(h) Hindrances to Prayer

_____

_____

_____

(i) The Results of Prayer

_____

_____

_____

It is well to make a trial division of the subject before taking up the individual passages given and to arrange each passage as we take it up under the appropriate heading. We may have to add to the divisions with which we began as we find new passages. The best classification of passages for any individual is the one he makes for himself, although he will get helpful suggestions from others.

IMPORTANT TOPICS

There are some subjects that every Christian should study and study as soon as possible. We give a list of these, in alphabetical order:

Adoption

Assurance

Atonement

Divine Healing

Faith

God: his Attributes and Work

Grace

Holiness

Justification

Life

Love

    - to all men

    - to God

    - to Jesus Christ

Messianic Prophecies

Peace

Perfection

Persecution

Prayer

    - answers to

    - intercessory

- praise
- private
- public
- social and family
- thanksgiving

Repentance

Sanctification

Sin

The Ascension of Christ

The Character of Christ

The Church

The Future Destiny of Believers

The Future Destiny of the Wicked

The Holy Spirit

- the Baptism of
- the Deity of
- the Fruit of
- the Gifts of
- the Personality of
- the Teacher

The Jews

The Judgments of God

The New Birth

The Reign of Christ

The Resurrection of Christ

The Second Coming of Christ

Water Baptism

CHAPTER STUDY

STUDY THE BIBLE BY CHAPTERS. This method of Bible study is not beyond any person of average intelligence who has fifteen minutes or more a day to put into Bible Study. It will take, however, more than one day to study a chapter if only fifteen minutes a day are set apart for the work;

(1) Select the chapters you wish to study. It is well to take a whole book and study the chapters in their order. The *Acts of the Apostles* (or the *Gospel of John)* is a good book to begin with. In time one may take up every chapter in the Bible, but it would not be wise to begin with *Genesis.*

(2) Read the chapter for today's study five times. It is well to read it aloud at least once. The writer sees many things when he reads the Bible aloud that he does not see when he reads silently. Each new reading will bring out some new point.

(3) Divide the chapters into their natural divisions and find headings for them that describe in the most striking way their contents. For example, suppose the chapter studied is *1 John 5*. You might divide it in this way:

1. *verses 1-3,* The Believer's Noble Parentage
2. *verses 4,5,* The Believer's Glorious Victory
3. *verses 6-10,* The Believer's Sure Ground of Faith
4. *verses 11,12,* The Believer's Priceless Possession
5. *verse 13,* The Believer's Blessed Assurance
6. *verses 14,15,* The Believer's Unquestioning Confidence
7. *verses 16,17,* The Believer's Great Power and Responsibility
8. *verses 18,19,* The Believer's Perfect Security
9. *verse 20,* The Believer's Precious Knowledge
10. *verse 21,* The Believer's Constant Duty

In many cases the natural divisions will be longer than in this chapter. Choose one of the *Psalms* (with no less than twelve verses), and on the dotted lines below, divide it into sections as in the above example.

_____

_____

_____

_____

_____

_____

(4) Note the important differences between the *Authorized Version* and modem versions. Add these to your notes for that verse.

(5) Note the leading facts of the chapter in their proper order.

(6) Make a note of the persons mentioned in the chapter and of any knowledge gained about their character. For example, if your chapter is *Acts 16,* then the persons mentioned are:

1. Timothy
2. Timothy's mother
3. Timothy's father
4. The brethren at Lystra and Iconium Paul
6. The Jews of Lystra and Iconium
7. The apostles and elders at Jerusalem
8. A man of Macedonia
9. Luke
10. Some women of Philippi
11. Lydia
12. The household of Lydia
13. A certain damsel possessed with a spirit of divination
14. The masters of this damsel
15. Silas
16. The praetors of Philippi
17. The Philippian mob
18. The gaoler of Philippi
19. The prisoners in the Philippian jail
20. The household of the gaoler
21. The lictors of Philippi
22. The brethren in Philippi

What does the chapter tell us about these characters?

(7) Note the principal lessons of the chapter. It would be well to classify these as *Lessons about:*

(a) *God*

(b) *Christ*

(c) *The Holy Spirit*

   - and so forth.

(8) The Central Truth of the chapter.

(9) The key verse of the chapter if there is one.

(10) The best verse in the chapter. Opinions will differ widely here. But the question is, which is the best verse to you at this present reading? Mark it and memorize it.

(11) Note the verses that are usable as texts for sermons or talks or Bible readings. If you have time make an analysis of the thought of these verses and record it.

(12) Name the chapter. For example,

   Acts 1 - The Ascension Chapter
   Acts 2 - The Day of Pentecost Chapter
   Acts 3- The Lame Man's Chapter
          and so forth.

Give your own names to the chapters. Give the name that sets forth the most important and characteristic feature of the chapter.

(13) Note subjects for further study. For example, you are studying Acts I. Subjects suggested for further study are:

   The Baptism with Holy Spirit
   The Second Coming of Christ.

(14) Words and phrases for further study. For example, if you are studying *John 3,* you should look up words and expressions such as:

   Eternal life,
   Born again,
   Water;
   Believer;
   The Kingdom of God.

(15) Note what new truth you have learned from the chapter. If you have learned none, you had better go over it again.

(16) What truth already known has come to you with new power?

(17) What definite thing have you resolved to do as a result of studying this chapter? A permanent record should be kept of the results of the study of each chapter.

THE WORD OF GOD

STUDY THE BIBLE AS THE WORD OF GOD. The Bible is the Word of God, and we get the most good out of any book by studying it for its true value. It is often said that we should study the Bible just as we study any other book. That principle contains a truth, but it also contains a great error. It is true that the Bible is a book as other books are, and the same laws of grammatical and literary construction and interpretation hold here as hold in other books. But the Bible is an entirely unique book. It is what no other book is - The Word of God. This can be easily proven to any candid man. The Bible ought then to be studied as no other book is. It should be studied as the Word of God. (I Th. 2:13) This involves five things -

(1) A greater *eagerness* and more *careful* and candid study to find out just what it teaches than is bestowed upon any other book or upon all other books. We must know the mind of God; here it is revealed.

(2) A prompt and unquestioning *acceptance* of and *submission* to its teachings when definitely ascertained, even when these teachings appear to us unreasonable or impossible. If this book is the Word of God how foolish to submit its teachings to the criticism of our finite reason. The little boy who discredits his wise father's statements because to his infant mind they appear unreasonable, is not a philosopher but a fool. When we are once satisfied that the Bible is the Word of God, its clear teachings must be the end of all controversy and discussion.

(3) Absolute *reliance* upon all its promises in all their length and breadth and depth and height. The one who studies the Bible as the Word of God will say of every promise no matter how vast and beyond belief it appears, *"God who cannot lie has promised this, so I claim it for myself"* Mark the promises you thus claim. Look each day for some new promise from your infinite Father. He has put *"his riches in glory"* at your disposal. ch 4:19)

(4) *Obedience* - prompt, exact, unquestioning, joyous obedience - to every command that is evident from the context that applies to you. Be on the lookout for new orders from the King. Blessing lies in the direct obedience to them. God's commands are but signboards that mark the road to present success and blessedness and to eternal glory.

(5) Studying the Bible as the *Word of God,* involves studying it as his own voice speaking directly to you. When you open the Bible to study it realize that you have come into the presence of God and that now he is going to speak to you. Every hour thus spent in Bible study will be an hour's walk and talk with God.

PRAYERFUL STUDY

STUDY THE BIBLE PRAYERFULLY. The author of the book is willing to act as interpreter of it. He does so when we ask him to. The one who prays with earnestness and faith, the Psalmist's prayer,

> "Open thou mine eyes that I may behold wondrous things out of thy law," -will get his eyes opened to see beauties and wonders in the Word that he never dreamed of before. Be very definite about this. Each time you open the Bible to study it, ask God to give you the open and discerning eye, and expect him to do it. Every time you come to a difficulty lay it before God and ask an explanation and expect it. How often we think as we puzzle over hard passages, "Oh if I only had so and so here to explain this." God is always present. Take it to him.

SEARCH FOR CHRIST

LOOK FOR "THE THINGS CONCERNING CHRIST... "IN ALL THE SCRIPTURES."

Christ is everywhere in the Bible (Luke 24:27) be on the lookout for him and mark his presence when you find it.

REDEEM THE TIME

IMPROVE SPARE MOMENTS IN BIBLE STUDY In almost every man's life many minutes each day are lost; while waiting for meals or buses, while riding in the car, etc. Carry a pocket Bible or Testament with you and save those golden minutes by putting them to the very best use listening to the voice of God. Print the topic your are studying (if you have a printer) so you can easily carry your notes with you.

MEMORISE THE TRUTH

STORE AWAY THE SCRIPTURE IN YOUR MIND AND HEART. It will keep you from sin (Ps 119:11,) from false doctrine (Ac 20:29,30,32 2Ti 3:13-15), it will fill you heart with joy (Je 15:16), and peace Ps 85:8), it will give you the victory over the Evil One (1 Jn 2:14), it will give you power in prayer (Jn 15:7), it will make you wiser than the aged and your enemies (Ps 119:100,98,130) it will make you "complete, furnished completely to every good work." (2 Ti 3:16,17) Try it. Do not memorize at random but memorize Scripture in a connected way. Memorize texts bearing on various subjects in proper order. Memorize by chapter and verse that you may know where to put your finger upon the text if any one disputes it.

ADDENDUM "A"

SAMPLE TOPICAL STUDIES[107]

(A) "ASSURANCE"

1) Prod uced by faith Ep3:12;2 Ti 1:12; He 10:22

2) Made full by hope Heb:11,19

3) Confirmed by love 1 Jn3:14,19;4:t8

4) Is the effect of righteousness Is 32:17

5) Is abundant in the understanding of the gospel Cl 2:2; 1 Th 1:5

6) SAINTS PRIVILEGED TO HAVE ASSURANCE OF -

   6a) Their election Ps 4:3; 1 Th 1:4

   6b) Their redemption Jb 19:25

   6c) Their adoption Ro 8:16; 1 Jn 3:2

   6d) Their salvation Is 12:2

   6e) Eternal life I Jn 5:13

   6f) The unalienable love of God Ro 8:38,39

   6g) Union with God and Christ I Co 6:15;2Co 13:5;Ep 5:30; 1 Jn 2:54:13

   6h) Peace with God by Christ Ro 5:1

   6i) Preservation Ps 3:6,8; 27:3-5; 46:1-3

   6j) Answers to prayer I Jn 3:22; 5:14,15

   6k) Continuance in grace Ph 1:6

---

107 The following Addenda were prepared by Ken Chant, using material from the *"On Line Bible"*

61) Comfort in affliction Ps 73:26; Lu 4:18,19; 2 Co 4:8-10,16-18

6m) Support in death Ps 23:4

6n) A glorious resurrection 3b 19:26; Ps 17:15; Ph 3:21; 1 Jn 3:2

6o) A kingdom He 12:28;Re5:l0

6p) A crown 2Ti 4:7,8;Ja 1:12

7) Give diligence to attain to2Pe 1:10,11

8) Strive to maintain He 3:14,18

9) Confident hope in God restores Ps 42:11

10) Exemplified in

10a) David Ps 23:4; 73:24-26

10b) Paul 2Ti 1:12;4:18

EXERCISE (A)

Select either *item 2* or *Item 5* above, write out the Bible texts, and then in your own words explain what they mean, and how they apply to your life-

_____

_____

_____

_____

_____

_____

_____

_____

_____

_____

_____

_____

_____

_____

_____

_____

_____

_____

_____

_____

_____

_____

_____

_____

EXERCISE (B)

"BAPTISM"

1)   As administered by John Mt 3:5-12; Jn 3:23; Ac 13:24; 19:4

2)   Sanctioned by Christ's submission to it Mt 3:13-15; Lu 3:21

3)   Adopted by Christ Jn 3:22; 4:1,2

4)   Appointed an ordinance of the Christian church Mt 28:19,20; Mk 16:15,16

5)   To be administered in the name of the Father, Son, and Holy Spirit Mt 28:19

6)   Water, the outward and visible sign in Ac 8:36; 10:47

7)   Regeneration, the inward and spiritual grace of Jn 3:3,5,6; Ro 6:3,4,11

8)   Remission of sins, signified by Ac 2:38 22:16

9) Unity of the Church effected by I Co 12:13; Ga 3:27,28

10) Confession of sin necessary to Mt 3:6

11) Repentance necessary to Ac 2:38

12) Faith necessary to Ac 8:37; 18:8

13) There is but one Ep 4:5

14) Administered to

14a) Individuals Ac 8:38; 9:18

14b) Households Ac 16:15; 1 Co 1:16

14c) Only to professing believers Ac 2:38; Mt 3:6; Mk 16:16: Ac 8:12,37; 10:47,48

14d) Scriptures supporting infant baptism Pr 30:6

15) Administered by immersing the whole body of the person in water Mt 3:16; Ac 8:38,39

16) Emblematic of the influences of the Holy Spirit Mt 3:11;Tit 3:5

17) Typified l Co 10:12, 1 I Pe 3:20,21

ADDENDUM "B"

SAMPLE VERSE STUDY

Text: Romans 5:1

Write out the text, and underline the key words.

_____

_____

_____

_____

_____

_____

_____

_____

_____

DEFINITIONS:

Using the definitions given below, and in the space provided, write out
the most appropriate meaning(s) each of the key words have in the above
text.   Note: while each definition in itself is correct, not all are
appropriate in every usage.

_1)_   _Therefore_: then, therefore, accordingly, consequently, these things
being so.

_____

_____

_____

_____

_____

_____

2) Justified:

    (a)   to render righteous or such as he ought to be;

    (b)   to show, exhibit, evince, one to be righteous, such as he is and wished himself to be considered;

    (c)   to declare, pronounce, one to be just, righteous, or such as he ought to be.

_____

_____

_____

_____

_____

3) _By_: a primary preposition denoting origin (the point whence action or motion proceeds), from, out (of place, time, or cause; literal or figurative; out of, from, by, away from.

_____

_____

_____

_____

_____

4) _Faith._

    (a) conviction of the truth of anything, belief; in the NT of a conviction or belief respecting man's relationship to God and divine things, generally with the included idea of trust and holy fervor born of faith and joined with it;

> (i) relating to God: the conviction that God exists and is the creator and ruler of all things, the provider and bestower of eternal salvation through Christ;

> (ii) relating to Christ: a strong and welcome conviction or belief that Jesus is the Messiah, through whom we obtain eternal salvation in the kingdom of God;

(b) the religious beliefs of Christians;

(c) belief with the predominate idea of trust (or confidence) whether in God or in Christ, springing from faith in the same;

(d) fidelity, faithfulness;

(e) the character of one who can be relied on.

_____

_____

_____

_____

_____

5) Have:

> (a) to have (hold) in the hand, in the sense of wearing, to have (hold) possession of the mind (refers to alarm, agitating emotions, etc.), to hold fast, to keep, to have or comprise or involve, to regard or consider or hold as;

> (b) to have i.e. own, possess;

> > (i) external things such as pertain to property or riches or furniture or utensils or goods or food etc.;

> > (ii) used of those joined to any one by the bonds of natural blood or marriage or friendship or duty or law etc, of attendance or companionship;

> (c) to hold one's self or find one's self so and so, to be in such or such a condition;

(d) to hold one's self to a thing, to lay hold of a thing, to adhere or cling to;

(e) to be closely joined to a person or a thing.

_____

_____

_____

_____

_____

6) Peace:

(a) a state of national tranquillity; exemption from the rage and havoc of war;

(b) peace between individuals, i.e. harmony, concord;

(c) security, safety, prosperity, felicity, (because peace and harmony make and keep things safe and prosperous);

(d) of the Messiah's peace; and of the way that leads to peace (salvation);

(e) of Christianity, the tranquil state of a soul assured of its salvation through Christ, and so fearing nothing from God and content with its earthly lot, of whatsoever sort that is;

(f) the blessed state of devout and upright people after death.

_____

_____

_____

_____

_____

7) *Through:* a primary preposition denoting the channel of an act;

(a) through;

    (i)   of place (with; in);

    (ii) of time (throughout; during);

    (iii) of means (by; by the means of);

b)   through; the ground or reason by which something is or is not done;

    (i)   by reason of;

    (ii) on account of;

    (iii) because of; for this reason;

    (iv) therefore;

    (v) on this account.

_____

_____

_____

_____

_____

ADDENDUM "C"

SAMPLE WORD STUDY

"FELLOWSHIP" (Greek, "koinonia")

Here are the 18 occurrences of this Greek word in the New Testament. Drawing from whichever of the definitions given below is appropriate, define the meaning of the underlined word(s) in each verse

_____

_____

_____

_____

Acts 2:42, "They devoted themselves to the apostles' teaching and fellowship, to the breaking of bread and the prayers.

_____

_____

_____

_____

Romans 15:26, "For Macedonia and Achaia have been pleased to share their resources with the poor among the saints at Jerusalem."

_____

_____

_____

_____

154

1 Corinthians 1:9, "God is faithful; by him you were called into the fellowship of his Son, Jesus Christ our Lord."

_____

_____

_____

_____

1 Corinthians 10:16, "The cup of blessing that we bless, is it not a sharing in the blood of Christ? The bread that we break, is it not a sharing in the body of Christ?"

_____

_____

_____

_____

_____

2 Corinthians 6:14, "Do not be mismatched with unbelievers. For what partnership is there between righteousness and lawlessness? Or what fellowship is there between light and darkness?"

_____

_____

_____

_____

2 Corinthians 8:4,"... begging us earnestly for the privilege of sharing in this ministry to the saints."

_____

_____

_____

_____

_____

2 Corinthians 9.13, "Through the testing of this ministry you glorify God by your obedience to the confession of the gospel of Christ and by the generosity of your <u>sharing</u> with them and with all others."

_____

_____

_____

_____

2 Corinthians 13:13 (14), "The grace of the Lord Jesus Christ, the love of God, and the <u>communion</u> of the Holy Spirit be with all of you."

_____

_____

_____

_____

Galatians 2:9, "When James and Cephas and John, who were acknowledged pillars, recognized the grace that had been given to me, they gave to Barnabas and me the right hand of <u>fellowship</u>, agreeing that we should go to the Gentiles and they to the circumcised."

_____

_____

_____

_____

Ephesians3:9, " . .. and to make everyone see what is the <u>plan</u> of the mystery hidden for ages in God who created all things."

_____

_____

_____

_____

Philippians 1:5, " ... because of your <u>sharing</u> in the gospel from the first day until now."

_____

_____

_____

_____

Philippians 2:1, "If then there is any encouragement in Christ, any consolation from love, any -<u>sharing</u> in the Spirit, any compassion and sympathy

_____

_____

_____

_____

Philippians 3:10, "I want to know Christ and the power of his resurrection and the <u>sharing</u> of his sufferings by becoming like him in his death."

_____

_____

_____

_____

Philemon 1:6, "I pray that the sharing of your faith may become effective when you perceive all the good that we may do for Christ."

_____

_____

_____

_____

Hebrews 13:16, "Do not neglect to do good and to share what you have, for such sacrifices are pleasing to God."

_____

_____

_____

_____

1 John 1:3, "We declare to you what we have seen and heard so that you also may have fellowship with us; and truly our fellowship is with the Father and with his Son Jesus Christ."

_____

_____

_____

_____

1 John 1:6.7, "If we say that we have fellowship with him while we are walking in darkness, we lie and do not do what is true; but if we walk in the light as he himself is in the light, we have fellowship with one another, and the blood of Jesus his Son cleanses us from all sin."

_____

_____

_____
_____
_____

DEFINITIONS

1)   fellowship, association, community, communion, joint participation, intercourse

    a)   the share which one has in anything, participation

    b)   intercourse, fellowship, intimacy

        i)   the right hand as a sign and pledge of fellowship (in fulfilling the apostolic office)

    c)   a gift jointly contributed, a collection, a contribution, as exhibiting an embodiment and proof of fellowship

2)   social, sociable, ready and apt to form and maintain communion and fellowship

3)   inclined to make others sharers in one's possessions, inclined to impart, free in giving, liberal

4)   a partner, associate, comrade, companion, sharer, in anything

    a)   of the altar in Jerusalem on which the sacrifices are offered

    b)   sharing in the worship of the Jews

    c)   partakers of (or with) demons; brought into fellowship with them, because they are the authors of heathen worship

APPLICATION

In the light of the above, what should be the characteristics of the "fellowship" that you share with your fellow Christians? Are you living close to this ideal? Write as comprehensive an answer as you can.

_____
_____
_____

OTHER BOOKS BY KEN & ALISON CHANT

Angelology
A study of the splendours of the heavenly realm

Attributes of Splendour
Reflections on the nature, being, and glory of God

Authenticity and Authority of the Bible
The Authenticity and Authority of scripture

Better than Revival
A Pragmatic look at Christian Ministry and the Idea of Revival

Building the Church God Wants
Not goal-setting, nor statistics, but faithfulness

Christian Life
A positive and creative approach to life.

Clothed with Power
A Pentecostal Theology of Holy Spirit baptism.

Corinthians
Studies in 1 Corinthians

Dazzling Secrets
The causes and the cure of depression for despondent saints.

Demonology
Understanding and overcoming our dark enemy

Discovery
Learning and living the will of God

Dynamic Christian Foundations
Studies in Foundational Christian Truths

Emmanuel 1

Jesus: Son of Man.

Emmanuel 2
Jesus: Man who is God.

Equipped To Serve
Understanding, receiving, & using the charismata to serve

Faith Dynamics
The limitless power of faith in God

Great Words of the Gospel
The major themes of salvation and holiness.

Healing in the New Testament
The healing covenant now.

Healing in the Old Testament
The healing covenant then.

Highly Exalted
The ascension and heavenly ministry of Christ

Mountain Movers
Secrets of mountain-moving prayer

Royal Priesthood
The priesthood of all believers.

Songs to Live By
Studies in the Psalms and Christian worship.

Strong Reasons
The Bible & Science, and the Proofs of God.

The Cross and the Crown
The passion and resurrection of Christ.

The Pentecostal Pulpit

The art of preaching in the power of the Holy Spirit.

The World's Greatest Story
The dramatic first millennium of church history

Throne Rights
Our position and spiritual authority in Christ.

Understanding Your Bible
Studies in biblical hermeneutics.

Unsung Heroines
Sage counsel for women in leadership in the church.

When the Trumpet Sounds
Studies in the Return of Christ.

Walking in the Spirit
The Apostle Paul offers as the key to successful
Christian living the instruction to, "Walk in the Spirit".

BIBLIOGRAPHY

Acts of King Arthur and His Noble Knights The; Ballantine Books, New York; 1990.

Adam Bede; George Eliot (1819-80).

Annotated Alice, The; Lewis Carroll; Bramhall House; New York, 1960.

Best of Robert Service, The; Robert Service; Dodd, Mead, & Co, New York, 1953.

Biblical Sermons; Ed. Haddon W. Robinson; Baker Book House; 1989.

Brief Lives; John Aubrey; The Folio Society, London 1975.

Canterbury Tales, The; Geoffrey Chaucer; tr. by Nevill Coghill; Penguin Classics, 1977.

Change Agent, The; Lyle E. Schaller; Abingdon Press; Nashville, 1986.

Children's Encyclopaedia; ed. Arthur Mee; Educational Book Society, London, 1963.

Christian Century, The; Art. by Anthony B. Robinson; Nov 3, 1993.

Christian Life; Ken Chant; Vision Publishing; Australia.

Christian Ministry Journal, The; Art. *Sermon Slips*, Nov-Dec 1988.

Chronicles of the Crusades; ed. Elizabeth Hallam; Weidenfeld and Nicolson, London, 1989.

Comedies, The; William Shakespeare; The Heritage Press; Norwalk, CT. 1986.

Creative Bible Teaching; Lawrence O. Richards; Moody Press; Chicago, 1971.

Effective Christian Ministry; Ronald W. Leigh; Tyndale House Publishers; Wheaton, Illinois, 1984.

Effective Speaking; Dale Carnegie; Morrison & Gibb; Kingswood, Surrey, 1962.

Evangelism and the Sovereignty of God; J. L. Packer.

Familiar Quotations, by John Bartlett; 1980.

First 40 Years, The; *Martin Lloyd-Jones;* Iaian H. Murray; Banner of Truth Trust, Edinburgh.

Five Comedies of Aristophanes; tr. Benjamin Bickley Rogers; Doubleday Anchor Books, New York, 1955.

French Revolution, The; Thomas Carlyle; The Folio Society; London, 1989.

Fuller's Worthies; Selected from, *The Worthies of England;* Thomas Fuller; ed. Richard Barber; The Folio Society; London, 1987.

Garden of the Prophet, The; Kahlil Gibran; Alfred A. Knopf, New York, 1986.

Grand Quarrel, The; ed. Roger Hudson; Folio Society, London, 1993.

Guide To Preaching, A; R. E. O. White; Pickering & Inglis Ltd.; London, 1973.

Happy Life; Martial (circa 40-104).

His Life As He Wrote It; Esmond Wright; Folio Society, London, 1989.

History of Alexander, The; *Book Five*, Quintus Curtius.

How Jesus Taught; Lilas D. Rixon; Sydney Missionary & Bible College; Croydon, NSW. 1977.

How To Prepare Bible Messages; James Braga; Multnomah Press; Portland, Oregon, 1969.

Inductive Preaching; Ralph L. Lewis with Gregg Lewis; Crossway Books; Westchester, Illinois, 1983.

Introduction to Homiletics, An; Donald E. Demaray Baker Book House; Grand Rapids, Michigan, 1974.

Jewish Literacy; Rabbi Joseph Telushkin; William Morrow & Co Inc, NY. 1991.

Le Morte d'Arthur; (1469) ed. R. M. Lumiansky; Collier MacMillan, London, 1986.

Lives of the Artists; Giorfio Vasari (1511-1574) tr. by George Bull; The Folio Society, London, 1993.

Matthew Henry's Commentary.

Meditations of Marcus Aurelius, The; tr. by Maxwell Staniforth; Penguin Books, 1986.

Nicene and Post-Nicene Fathers, The; *Second Series, Vol. Six* (1892) Eerdmans Pub. Co., reprint of the original; 1979.

No Proper Name; W. E. Best; published by the author.

Olympian Odes, II, l. 150; Pindar (circa 518 – 483 B.C.).

Online Bible, The;. *Methods of Bible Study*; R. A. Torrey.

Perils of Persuasive Preaching, The; A. Duane Litfin, Art. *Christianity Today Magazine*, February 4, 1977.

Pillow Book, The; Sei Shonagon; Tr. Ivan Morris; Penguin Classics; 1967.

Poems of Robert Browning, The; ed. C. Day Lewis; The Heritage Press; Norwalk, Connecticut, 1971.

Poor Richard's Almanac; Benjamin Franklin; 1746.

Public Speaking & Influencing Men In Business; Dale Carnegie; Windmill Press; Kingswood, Surrey, 1951.

Pythian Odes, IV, l. 510; Pindar (circa 518 - circa 438 B.C.)

Ruba'iyat of Omar Khayyam,The; tr. by Avery & Heath-Stubbs; Penguin Classics, 1983.

Sirach – The Apocrypha.

Solitude; *St. One*; Ella Wheeler Wilcox (1850-1919).

Songs To Live By; Ken Chant; Vision Christian College, Sydney, 1994.

Table Talk of Martin Luther; ed. Thomas Kepler, Baker Book House, 1979.

Teach or Perish; James De Forest Murch; William B. Eerdman's Pub. Grand Rapids, Michigan, 1967.

Tess of the D'Urbervilles; Thomas Hardy (1891) The Folio Society, London, reprint 1991.

Week On The Concord and Merrimac Rivers, A; The Heritage Press, CT, 1975 edition;

What Luther Says; compiled by Ewald M. Plass; Concordia Publishing House, St Louis,1959.

Yes, You Can Teach; Julie Wayner; Aglow Publications; Lynnwood WA. 1977.

Your Preaching; A Force or a Farce; John Deane.

www.ingramcontent.com/pod-product-compliance
Lightning Source LLC
Chambersburg PA
CBHW052344090426
42739CB00011B/2305